Comments on Grant Je[illegible]
14 *best-selling book[illegible]*

ARMAGEDDON	•	MESSIAH
APOCALYPSE	•	THE PRINCE OF DARKNESS
FINAL WARNING	•	THE SIGNATURE OF GOD
HEAVEN	•	THE HANDWRITING OF GOD
MILLENNIUM MELTDOWN	•	PROPHECY STUDY BIBLE
FLEE THE DARKNESS	•	BY DAWN'S EARLY LIGHT
MYSTERIOUS BIBLE CODES	•	JESUS: THE GREAT DEBATE

"Grant Jeffrey has written an extraordinary new book, ***The Signature of God***, that provides astonishing proof that the Bible was inspired by God. Grant is recognized as the leading researcher in Bible Prophecy today." *Hal Lindsey, Hal Lindsey Ministries*

"The ***Prophecy Study Bible*** is a phenomenal publishing effort by one of America's premier prophecy experts. Comprehensive, understandable, and powerful. A great work!"

Dr. Ed. Hindsen, Editor – Jesus Study Bible

"The ***Prophecy Study Bible*** is the most comprehensive, contemporary, and in-depth study of the most relevant prophecies in the Bible — A must addition to every serious student of the Word of God."

Dr. Chuck Missler – Koinonia House Ministries

"***Prince of Darkness*** was written by acclaimed Bible Prophecy teacher Grant R. Jeffrey. This unequaled masterpiece is the result of 30 years of intense research. It will stir you and inspire you as few books have. . . . It is extremely well written — extraordinarily researched and fascinatingly presented . . . this is the best book I have ever read on this subject." *Dr. Jack Van Impe, Jack Van Impe Ministries*

"***Armageddon: Appointment With Destiny*** has been our hottest single religious title. . . . We took it on with tremendous enthusiasm because there was something very exciting about the way Grant wrote, and it was something that we thought might go beyond the traditional religious audience." *Lou Arnonica, Vice President, Bantam Books, New York Times, October 22, 1990*

"We are excited about Grant Jeffrey's new book. . . . Now the book with the latest information on prophetic fulfilment, the book of the nineties, is ***Armageddon: Appointment With Destiny***. It will show that God is in control and, most importantly, it will also prove to be a powerful witnessing tool to those who need Christ."

David Mainse: Host, 100 Huntley Street

Journey Into Eternity

Search For Immortality

Dr. Grant R. Jeffrey

Frontier Research Publications, Inc.
P.O. Box 129, Station "U", Toronto, Ontario M8Z 5M4

Journey Into Eternity

Library of Congress Cataloging in Publication Data:
Jeffrey, Dr. Grant R.
Journey Into Eternity
1. Prophecy 2. Heaven 3. Near Death Experiences
1. Title

August 2000 Frontier Research Publications, Inc.

ISBN 0-921714-60-2

Unless otherwise indicated, Scripture quotations are from the Authorized King James Version.

Cover design: The Riordon Design Group
Printed in Canada: Harmony Printing Limited

Table of Contents

Acknowledgments

Journey Into Eternity — Search For Immortality is an exploration of the scientific, medical, philosophical, and Scriptural evidence about the question of life after death. One of the most important chapters in the book is the examination of the evidence that proves that Jesus of Nazareth truly died and then rose from the dead. The information provided by Jesus Christ Himself on the nature of the soul's condition after death is vital if we are to understand what awaits all of us on "the other side of Jordan." This book is the result of over thirty-five years of research involving thousands of books, scientific and medical articles, interviews, and Bible commentaries.

The Scriptures and their statements about the reality and nature of the afterlife are subject to continuous attack in our generation in the universities, the liberal seminaries, and the media. Yet our faith as Christians and our personal confidence of salvation as we ourselves face death is based ultimately on the truthfulness and trustworthiness of the sacred Scriptures. While this book contains fascinating research and documentation about the latest scientific and medical experiments, deathbed visions, and near death experiences, the only reliable information about the nature of our future spiritual life is revealed in the inspired words of Scripture. Our Christian faith is based on the life, death, and resurrection of Jesus Christ. As this book demonstrates, our faith is grounded upon a strong foundation of historical fact that proves beyond a shadow of a doubt that Jesus of Nazareth rose from the dead.

My parents, Lyle and Florence Jeffrey, have continuously inspired in me a profound love for Jesus Christ and His revelation of truth in the Word of God. They continue to encourage me in my research and writing.

A very special thanks to my editorial assistant, Adrienne Jeffrey Tigchelaar, who has provided valuable research and editorial services throughout this project.

Journey Into Eternity is dedicated to my loving wife, Kaye, who is my constant inspiration, my faithful partner in ministry, and the Vice President of Frontier Research Publications, Inc. As we travel the world together to conduct research and minister in various nations, she continually encourages me in my efforts to share this research through my writing and teaching.

I trust that the information revealed in the following pages will encourage you to personally study the Bible's truth about life, death, and the hope of resurrection.

Dr. Grant R. Jeffrey
Toronto, Ontario
June, 2000

1

Introduction

Does our life end forever when we die, or will we live again? If we do live again, what will be the nature of our existence after this life? And if we do live again, will we retain our memories, and our personal identity from this life? These questions arise in the minds of almost every one of us when we contemplate our own death. This book will explore the question of immortality in light of the medical and scientific discoveries of the last several decades, and powerful truths revealed in the Scriptures. The evidence will demonstrate that our soul does survive after the death of our body and that we are all on a personal journey into eternity.

Over three and a half thousand years ago Job struggled with the issue of immortality when he asked the profound question that faces each of us: "If a man die, shall he live again?" (Job 14:14). The answer to this enduring question has perplexed humans for thousands of years. Anyone who seriously considers the issue of the eternal destiny of our soul must seek the answer to these vital questions: Do we simply live our allotted span of seventy to eighty years and then expire forever? Or, has God implanted in our spirit a sense of our own spiritual immortality and a longing for eternity to teach us that our immortal spirits were created to live in two worlds — this temporary earthly world, and then, the eternal life to come?

This profound question has troubled the hearts and minds of all people in every nation, culture, and religion throughout history. The question of what happens to us after death has provoked discussion and debate in all societies. We instinctively recoil from the idea that our life and identity will end forever when our body is finally laid to rest in the grave. Every one of us stands each hour on the razor's edge between the mortal and the immortal. Each moment we face the issues of life, death, and eternity — subject at any time to be removed from the one state into the other. Can we discover the truth and demonstrate that the human spirit continues to consciously exist after the body has died?

Many questions naturally occur when we consider life, death, and immortality. What is death? Why must we die? Will we live again after we die? Does our consciousness cease forever when our physical body stops breathing and returns to the dust from which we came? If we do live forever, what is the nature of our immortal life? Is there a judgment and reward after this life is over? What happens to us immediately after we die? Will we be aware of those still left on earth? Is there really a Heaven to yearn for and a Hell to fear?

It is significant that the oldest book in the Bible, the book of Job, addresses this vital question, "If a man die, shall he live again?" There is no other philosophical or religious question that could possibly be more fascinating or ultimately more important to each of us than the question of the final destiny of our conscious soul following our death. It is only natural to pause momentarily when a funeral procession passes and ponder the eternal question: "Someday my body also will be placed in the grave, but what will happen to *Me*? What will happen to my soul?"

If we should encounter a person who had actually died and returned to life to reveal the truth about what happens to the spirits of all humans, both those who repent of their sins and those who reject God's mercy, what questions would we ask of them?

Perhaps the following questions would occur to many of us:

- What did it feel like to die?
- Were you conscious of your soul leaving your body after death?
- What occurred at the very moment of death?
- What did you experience in the moments immediately following your death?
- Did you encounter angelic beings at the moment of death?
- What was the nature of your spiritual body after death?
- Did you personally see Jesus or God?
- Did you recognize anyone after death that you knew in your earthly life?
- What is the truth about Heaven, Hell, or the condition of the departed spirits after death?

Throughout this book we will explore intriguing research from nature, medicine, science, and psychology, that indicates that our personal consciousness does indeed survive the death of our body. Experiments in which hamsters have died in a laboratory and returned to life after four hours raise provocative questions about the reality and last moments of death. Medical reports about the clinical death of patients who later returned to life after a prolonged period with no brain function or life signs raise additional questions about when death actually occurs and whether our spirit may be able to exist for some time independently of our physical body. Finally we will reach a point where philosophy, medicine, nature, and science have revealed their truths — all pointing to the strong probability that our individual consciousness does survive death. But can we have a greater assurance beyond probability? Fortunately, when nature and science are finally silent, the voice of God speaks clearly to us through His written revelation, recorded over the span of sixteen centuries by forty-four human authors and inspired by God's Holy Spirit — the Bible.

Ultimately, what we need is a written testimony from someone who has truly died and then returned from the grave to tell us about the nature of life after death. Jesus of Nazareth claims to be the one person who died, rose from the grave, and now declares the truth about our immortal life. Jesus rose from the empty tomb on the third day following his death to announce that He had defeated death and the grave forever. We will examine the claims of Jesus Christ regarding His death and resurrection to establish the truth of His unique claim. Then we will explore in depth His written revelations about the nature of our eternal life in either Heaven or Hell.

The written revelation of the Bible is the only reliable source of information that clearly illuminates the final truth about our soul's purpose and our eternal destiny. We willingly sit at the feet of poets, medical doctors, research scientists, and philosophers to learn whatever they can reveal about immortality, but in the end, the inspired Word of God will prove to be our most reliable instructor and our final court of appeal regarding the truth about life after death and the way to the gates of Heaven.

Death is the final crisis on earth for each of us. Philosophical and religious writings of ancient cultures, as well as the more sophisticated writings of many modern philosophers and theologians, agree that there is a God who created humanity with a divine purpose and that man was created to live forever in an immortal relationship with God Almighty in Heaven. The scientific evidence of the masterful and purposeful design revealed in nature strongly suggests to the unbiased mind that a Supreme Intelligence must have created the marvelous order evident in our world. The God who created this universe obviously also created the spiritual dimension of humanity.

Every minute of each day we stand on a sharp precipice between life and death — between mortality and immortality — the known and the unknown. In light of the obvious fact that every one of us must someday face the crisis of our human mortality at some point in time, we need to carefully consider the vital question of whether the moment of our death is the final and complete end of our conscious existence. Or, is that moment of our death only the beginning of a potentially glorious new experience that will transcend our normal earthly existence as the brilliant, warm light of a new dawn replaces the cold, darkness of the long night that came before.

The almost universal existence of a profound desire for immortality in virtually all cultures provides powerful, presumptive evidence that life after death is, in fact, a reality. A Gallup poll at the beginning of the 1980s surveyed

Americans to determine their beliefs regarding the afterlife. Interestingly, 71 percent of those surveyed declared that they believed in Heaven while only 21 percent believed in Hell; the balance was unsure. Intriguingly, 67 percent of Americans surveyed expressed a strong belief in life after death.[1]

When we consider the question of whether or not life ends forever at our physical death, we are confronted with the mystery of why virtually all humans who mourn at the death of their loved ones feel a strong emotion of deep loss and a profound yearning to be reunited in an afterlife with their deceased loved ones. For those who suggest that there is no life beyond the present one, consider the millions who weep at the graveside, sincerely believing that their loved ones still exist in some other place.

Obviously, as long as people die, humans will continually be confronted with the profound question: Can evidence support the notion that the human soul survives death? While this question has been asked for thousands of years, it remains among the most important questions that we face as humans. Our death is not something common simply because it happens to every human. Our own death will be a unique experience because it will be totally unprecedented for each of us.

Why should we consider the question of the immortality of the soul? The truth is that we cannot ignore the question of the possibility of our survival of physical death anymore than we can ignore the issue of human life or love itself. The ancient Greek philosopher Democritus stated, "The soul is the house of God." The modern writer Martineau wisely wrote, "We do not believe in immortality because we have proved it, but we forever try to prove it because we believe it." Another writer, Theodore Parker, correctly noted, "All men desire to be immortal."

The great English writer, Alfred, Lord Tennyson, wrote about the universal longing for immortality:

No life that breathes with human breath
Has ever truly longed for death.

The brilliant American statesman and philosopher Benjamin Franklin discussed the matter of his approaching death and his personal belief in the afterlife with a friend just before the end of his life. Franklin confidently affirmed,

> Death is as necessary to the constitution as sleep; we shall rise refreshed in the morning. The course of nature must soon put a period to my present mode of existence. This I shall submit to with the less regret, as, having seen, during a long life, a good deal of this world, I felt a growing curiosity to become acquainted with some other, and can cheerfully, with filial confidence, resign my spirit to the conduct of that great and good Parent of mankind who created it, and who has so graciously protected and preserved me from my birth to the present hour.[2]

Some people suggest that any philosophical question such as immortality that cannot be *scientifically proven* to everyone's complete and immediate satisfaction should be completely ignored as unworthy of serious consideration. However, this approach rejects the Western legal tradition of evaluating controversial evidence in a court of law before twelve neutral citizens. Our courts routinely consider and pass serious judgments, including death sentences, in cases in which the conclusion of the jury or the judge must inevitably depend upon both logical deduction and circumstantial evidence.

The agnostic philosophy that refuses to consider even the possibility of a future spiritual life after death such as Heaven or Hell is often expressed by the thought that *one world at a time is enough*. The subject of atheism is virtually ignored in the Scriptures. There are no passages in the Bible that discuss the question of whether or not God exists. In fact, the Scriptures do not take the trouble to debate the assertions of atheists who reject the existence of God and our eternal soul. The only passage in the Holy Scriptures that addresses the question of atheism at all is found in one of the Psalms written by King David: "The fool hath said in his heart, There is no God." (Psalms 14:1) The Bible dismisses the pretense of atheism as an obviously invalid belief. King David longed for the time when he would enter into Heaven and enjoy the presence of his beloved God forevermore. David wrote, "For a day in thy courts is better than a thousand. I had rather be a door keeper in the house of my God, than to dwell in the tents of wickedness" (Psalms 84:10).

The ancient catechism of the Church poses the question of man's ultimate purpose in God's creation: "What is the chief end of Man?" The written answer was: "Man's chief end is to glorify God, and enjoy Him forever." This statement expresses the virtually universal understanding of past generations in western Europe that an intimate and powerful relationship exists between God and humanity. The expectation of a Heavenly afterlife is the natural result of a life of faith in the Lordship of Jesus Christ. This understanding of the all-encompassing and eternal relationship between mankind and God is expressed by the well-known verse, "Whether therefore ye eat or drink, or whatsoever ye do do all to the glory of God" (1 Corinthians 10:31).

God reveals Himself in His Creation as a God of power. He also reveals Himself as a God of wisdom in His manifest providence to us. The revelation of His law throughout the Scriptures reveals His divine justice as well. Finally, He reveals Himself as a God of love. The invitation of Christ remains open to anyone who will reject their sinful pride and accept His offer of salvation and His welcome into Paradise. The knowledge of our final triumph over death and the grave through Christ can liberate us from the fear of death.

We will also examine evidence from the world of nature, philosophy, religion, personal experience, medicine, and science about life after death, and finally, the written declarations about the reality of the resurrection body of Jesus of Nazareth. I believe that the evidence will provide ample proof that we are destined to live forever. Furthermore, the evidence will show that those who have faith in Jesus Christ will live forever in a glorious resurrection body similar to His own, after He rose victorious over the grave. The resurrection of Jesus Christ from the garden tomb robbed death of its previous triumph over life. The Gospels declare Christ's victory over death for all who place their faith in Him: "O Death where is thy sting, O Grave, where is thy victory?"(1 Corinthians 15:55).

From the moment we are born, every one of the trillions of cells that make up our human body begin to die. At the time of our birth every single human embarks on a personal journey through life and then death until we achieve our eternal spiritual home. The moment of our death is a point of transition along this journey into eternity. For those who place their faith in Christ, this journey will culminate in

God's promise of a glorious resurrection body and the New Jerusalem in Heaven.

Notes

1. G. Gallup, Jr., and W. Proctor, *Adventures in Immortality* (New York: McGraw Hill, 1982).
2. J. E. Stebbins, *Our Departed Friends of Glory of the Immortal Life* (Hartford: L. Stebbins, 1867).

2

Universal Belief in Immortality

To see a world in a grain of sand
And a Heaven in a wild flower,
Hold infinity in the palm of your hand
And eternity in an hour.[1]

William Blake

Perhaps the strongest evidence supporting the truth of immortality is that virtually every tribe, nation, and culture throughout history has expressed a strong faith in the reality of a life after death. In addition to the almost universal belief in God, the conviction that we will live again after our earthly bodies return to dust is the strongest and most commonly held belief of humanity. For thousands of years the vast majority of people have approached their personal valley of death with the firm expectation that they will ultimately rise from death and live forever in a better world. The longing for eternal life is the strongest instinct found in the heart of every human.

How can anyone contemplate the river of humanity that flows constantly toward an open grave that will finally encompass every one of us without asking the ultimate question: Where will our souls go? What will happen to these millions of mothers, fathers, sons, and daughters who were once so full of life, plans, hopes, and dreams? The problem of death and the question of what will happen to our soul after death remains the most profound and important question facing every one of us.

It is natural, when we are young, to ignore the risk of death and foolishly act as if we will live forever. Much of the foolishness and wildness in the actions of young people is a result of their natural tendency to dismiss the risk of serious pain or death due to their inability to conceive of the final certainty of their own departure. Studies of the beliefs of children, however, reveal that a majority of young people believe in immortality and the continuation of life after death. Surely the truth of immortality speaks to us through the witness of children as they face loss of life with a confidence in their soul's survival in the open arms of their heavenly Father.

Evidence from the anthropologists who have studied the traditions and religious beliefs of thousands of cultures confirms that belief in immortality and a pleasing afterlife for the souls of the virtuous is almost universal. The concept of immortality, however, was generally vague and often contradictory during ancient times. Frequently immortality was intermingled with pagan notions of multiple gods and goddesses. For example, a Chinese Buddhist scripture declares, "Man never dies. The soul inhabits the body for a time, and leaves it again. The soul is myself: the body is only my dwelling place. Birth is not birth: there is a soul already existent when the body comes to it. Death is not death: the soul merely departs, and the body falls. It's because men see only their bodies that they love life and hate death." However, the fact that every culture and nation developed such concepts regarding the soul's survival provides compelling evidence that the desire for an immortal spiritual life is strongly rooted in the soul of humanity. While these strong prevailing beliefs about immortality do not provide actual proof, they do provide compelling evidence that God created humanity with a vacuum in our spirits that can only be fulfilled with the belief that we were purposely created to enjoy an eternal and purposeful spiritual existence with Him.

While specific religious ideas often vary widely in their expression, the two complementary beliefs that God exists and that our soul is immortal have been universally taught by both ancient and medieval philosophers. The Roman writer Cicero wrote, "In everything the consent of all nations is to be accounted the law of nature, and to resist it is to resist the voice of God."

The Greek writer Phocylides wrote, "Immortal souls, free from old age, live forever. . . . All the dead are equal, but God governs souls." The great ancient Greek authors including Homer, Ovid, and Virgil all taught that the sages of past centuries believed both in God's existence and in an eternal afterlife where good souls were rewarded and evil was punished. Homer wrote,

Tis true, tis certain; man, though dead, retains
Part of himself: the immortal mind remains;
The form subsists without the body's aid,

Aerial semblance, and an empty shade.

Socrates, the great Greek philosopher of Athens, remarked on the question of immortality according to his students. He said, "I cannot find it in me to disbelieve so probable and desirable a truth." The philosopher Plato also suggested that the passion of love produces a profound longing for eternity and therefore justifies our belief that our loved ones must still exist in another plane of existence. At the most exalted level of love, there is a perception that our consciousness and love will transcend time to exist forever. A powerful component of true love is that it naturally longs for the continuation of the passionate joy of both the relationship and the life of the beloved.

The Scriptures affirm that God created humanity in His own image for His own purpose. Therefore it is logical to assume that He has given us a fundamental and instinctive understanding that our souls were created for an eternal spiritual purpose. The spiritual nature of humans, the holiness of our Divine Creator, and the necessity of eternal justice requires a continuation of our human souls. Survival would allow for both eternal reward for righteous deeds for those who seek God's forgiveness and punishment for those who rebelliously reject God's offer of pardon of man's sins.

The young poet Byron arrogantly expressed his personal contempt for the concept of immortality when he declared, "I will have nothing to do with your Immortality; we are miserable enough in this life, without the absurdity of speculating upon another." However, later in his life, a more mature and wiser Byron wrote the following poem, indicating that his progress of years had effected a change in his opinion.

I feel my immortality o'ersweeps
All pains, all tears, all time, all fears and peals
Like the eternal thunders of the deep,
Into my ears this truth, — 'Thou liv'st forever.'
George Byron (1788–1824)

Many religions share the belief that all those who rise from the dead will retain their personal identity and physical appearance during the intermediate state between death and the final moment of bodily resurrection from the grave, allowing recognition by friends and family. This belief is supported by the teaching of Jesus Christ in His parable about the afterlife regarding the destiny of the righteous beggar and the unrepentant rich man. In addition, it is fascinating to note that three of Christ's disciples identified Moses and Elijah when they appeared in their supernatural bodies with Jesus on the Mount of Transfiguration.

Some skeptics reject belief in immortality because they erroneously believe that this concept is a mere superstition arising solely from ancient religions such as Christianity or Judaism. Since they distrust religion generally, they automatically reject belief in the afterlife of the soul without truly considering the real evidence for or against immortality. These skeptics contemptuously reject the opinions of those who express a personal spiritual faith because they assume that religious minds must have a profound bias in favor of immortality that must make their conclusions suspect. However, it is equally obvious that an atheist will impart just as strong a bias against belief in immortality. The real question to be addressed by any impartial observer is this: Which of these opposing biases is more likely to interfere with an objective search for the truth about the question of immortality? Some skeptics reject the possibility of life after death in the mistaken belief that immortality is only an artificial doctrine created by society and religion to coerce men and women to live virtuous lives in the hope of Heaven and the fear of Hell. They suggest that mature humans do not need such inducements to motivate them to live virtuous lives.

Agnostics reject immortality partially because the subject of life after death is impossible to absolutely prove beyond a reasonable doubt, therefore leaving us with only possibilities and probabilities rather than scientific certainties.

The agnostics claim that since the spiritual world is basically inaccessible, the question of the life of our soul after death is therefore unknowable and thus unworthy of serious inquiry. Since modern science confines itself to those things that can be observed and confirmed by other scientists, the question of life after death seems to lie outside the field of normal science. Therefore, the skeptics suggest we should ignore the question of immortality because we can never know with absolute certainty whether or not life exists beyond the grave. The agnostic declares that the only reasonable answer to the question of whether our soul can survive beyond death is, "We cannot know."

The Scottish writer Thomas Carlyle wrote about the apparent silence of the grave: "Thousands of generations, all as noisy as our own, have been swallowed up of time, and there remains no wreck of them any more, and Pleiades, and Arcturus, and Orion, and Sirus, are still shining in their courses, clear young as when the shepherd first noted them on the plains of Shinar."[2]

Many scientists reject the possibility of life after death on the basis that the physical destruction of the body and brain following death eliminates the possibility that our mind or conscious identity could survive. Since our consciousness, our memory, our identity, and our mental processes obviously depend upon the instantaneous electrical-chemical interactions of trillions of complex nerve cells within our physical brain it is logical to conclude that the destruction of the physical brain must inevitably terminate our mental and spiritual consciousness forever.

However, we know that many times in life appearances are deceiving. For example, it appears as if the sun rises in the east every morning and sets in the west every night. Yet centuries ago that apparent fact was proven to be erroneous when scientists used telescopes to prove that the earth was actually revolving around the sun. In a later chapter we will examine several scientific experiments that strongly suggest that our soul does survive after death.

Another example is that, to all natural appearances, when we stand outside we seem to be standing perfectly still. Yet, according to astronomers, we are actually moving rapidly on the surface of this revolving planet in the northern latitudes at the rate of approximately 900 miles an hour. In addition, the earth itself is rapidly orbiting around our sun at a speed greater than 22,000 miles an hour. Meanwhile, our earth, the entire solar system, and our enormous Milky Way galaxy, which has more than 200 billion stars, is traveling at an enormous velocity through space in the generally northern direction across the plane of the galactic disk on an inconceivable long journey toward the region of the distant star known as Vega. It is impossible to calculate the earth's precise velocity as we travel through interstellar space because there is no absolutely stationary object against which our relative speed can be compared. However, the great disparity between our natural perception that we are stationary in comparison to the proven scientific fact that we are actually traveling at an astonishing speed through space proves that our natural perceptions cannot always be trusted.

Unfortunately, many thoughtful people have rejected any serious consideration of the question of immortality of our soul on the basis that absolute scientific proof of immortality of the human spirit is unobtainable. Therefore, they conclude that any further consideration of the question of the survival of the human spirit after death is pointless. However, this naive approach, to reject every bit of evidence on a subject unless it can be established to a degree of absolute scientific certainty, is simply false reasoning. That rigid approach to the search for truth would force us to eliminate our complete judicial system.

Every day judges and juries reach serious conclusions that affect the lives of defendants based on a preponderance of evidence that establishes a strong probability that the accused either committed the crime or that he should be acquitted of the charge. Throughout our life we are constantly forced to decide important and vital issues based on a weight of probabilities instead of an illusive scientific certainty that is usually unavailable. In the vast majority of cases, scientific evidence that is incontrovertible and provides absolute certainty is not available to us when we must make important decisions. Therefore, when we consider this question of immortality, we must finally decide on the basis of the weight of the evidence and the probability that the evidence points one way or another.

The scientific study of nature reveals that God has created millions of species of animals, birds, and insects with special instincts to attract them toward the appropriate food, shelter, and mates that are essential to their survival. More than two centuries of scientific observation has revealed that there is not one known example of a creature that possesses an instinct to seek for something that does not exist. In every known case the instinct of the creature is matched with a corresponding object. If humanity was created with a profound longing for immortality, and eternal life should ever be proven not to exist, this would be the only example in all of nature where a species has an instinctual longing for something that does not actually exist. In light of this universal observation, the fact that humanity everywhere longs instinctively for life after death provides the strongest possible evidence that our spirits were created by God to live forever.

Whether it is a close call with death through an averted accident, or the death of a close friend or beloved relative, every one of us at some time in our life comes to a realization that we are truly mortal — that someday each of us will finally die. If humans were created by God to enjoy immortality, an understanding of this future existence from both a biblical and evidential basis can have profound significance for us in this life.

Like many young people, the English poet William Cowper, in the full exuberance of his earthly life, was contemptuous of death. He acted and spoke as though he would never taste of death. Yet one night, as he was walking home, he found himself passing through the churchyard and cemetery of St. Margaret's church. A grave digger who was digging a new grave that night inadvertently threw a skull from an old grave out onto the path in front of Cowper. His confrontation with that skull on his midnight walk awakened within the poet an impending sense of his own mortality. The appearance of the skull reminded Cowper that the owner of this skull was once as full of life as himself. This chance event arrested and transformed Cowper's thoughts with the belated realization that he, like the rest of humanity, must someday pass through the portals of death and give a final account to his Maker.

The American philosopher, Ralph Waldo Emerson, known as the sage of Concord, wrote about "man's audacious belief in a future life." Emerson also wrote about the universal nature of this belief in life after death, "In the minds of all men, or wherever man appears, this belief appears with him, in the savage savagely, in the pure purely." Later Emerson wrote, "Our dissatisfaction with any other solution is the blazing evidence of immortality." Another famous poet, Longfellow, wrote about his personal conviction regarding life after death as follows: "The grave itself is but a covered bridge leading from light to light through a brief, darkness." Even the poet Alfred, Lord Tennyson declared his conviction regarding our immortality.

For tho' from out our bourne of Time and Place
The flood may bear me far,
I hope to see my Pilot face to face
When I have crossed the Bar.

Alfred, Lord Tennyson (1809–1892)

A number of great authors have written about their personal belief in life eternal. Several excerpts taken from their various works illustrate their thoughts about immortality.

But at my back I always hear
Time's winged chariot hurrying near;
And yonder all before us lie
Deserts of vast eternity.

Andrew Marvell: *To His Coy Mistress*

Is this the end? I know it cannot be,
Our ships shall sail upon another sea;

New islands yet shall break upon our sight,
New continents of love and truth and might.
John White Chadwisk

Oh, may I join the choir invisible
Of those immortal dead who live again.
George Eliot: *The Choir Invisible*

We cannot resist the conviction that
this world is for us only the porch of another and
more magnificent temple of the creator's majesty.
Frederick William Faber

The poet Joseph Addison wrote about the hope of immortality and the instinctive revulsion all humans feel for the thought that our life might end in the annihilation of our soul.

It must be so, Plato, thou reason'st well,
Else whence this pleasing hope, this fond desire,
This longing after immortality?
Or whence this secret dread and inward horror
Of falling into nought?
Why shrinks the soul
Back on herself and startles at destruction?
'Tis the divinity that stirs within us,
'Tis Heaven itself that points out a hereafter,
And intimates eternity to man.
Joseph Addison (1672–1719)

Immortality and the Problem of Injustice

Anyone who considers the great injustices and evil that apparently receives no adequate judgment in this world must naturally wonder about the claim that we live in a universe of justice and reward for good deeds. The truth is that very often in this life evil deeds appear to be rewarded with wealth and success. Equally true is the observation that good deeds often are ignored and sometimes even generate negative responses from ungrateful people.

As we read our daily newspapers or watch the evening news, we are often appalled at the growing injustice that surrounds us. Almost every day brings new reports of evil and powerful people who elude the law and disprove the proverb "Crime doesn't pay." Meanwhile billions of innocent people go hungry and often lose their homes and employment in waves of natural disasters. Our heart rebels against the injustice that our eyes observe. Many cry out to God, "Where is the justice?" King Solomon was the wisest man who ever lived. Yet Solomon also struggled with the same dilemma that faces every one of us. He wrote, "I returned and saw under the sun that the race is not to the swift, nor the battle to the strong, nor bread to the wise, nor riches to men of understanding, nor favor to men of skill, but time and chance happen to them all" (Ecclesiastes 9:11). Solomon then pondered the ultimate judgment that awaits each of us in eternity: "I said in my heart, God shall judge the righteous and the wicked: for there is a time there for every purpose and for every work" (Ecclesiastes 3:17). But Solomon ultimately ends his deliberations in confidence that God would ultimately judge all souls appropriately: "Let us hear the conclusion of the whole matter: Fear God, and keep His commandments: For this is man's all. For God will bring every work into judgment, including every secret thing, Whether good, or evil" (Ecclesiastes 12:13,14).

Repeatedly the Bible proclaims that God will ultimately judge every deed and motive of both humans and angels. True justice will finally be rendered, but, thankfully, the justice of God is offered to us in combination with His mercy.

God's incomparable mercy is manifested to us in Christ's offered gift of salvation to anyone who will repent of their sinful rebellion and accept Jesus as their personal Savior. As John Milton wrote in his magnificent poem *Paradise Lost*, the rebellious choice of Satan and every lost soul who rejects Christ's offer of salvation is really this: "My choice to reign is worth ambition though in Hell: Better to reign in Hell, than serve in Heaven."

Once we arrive at a firm conclusion that our souls are destined to live forever, it is vital that we determine the nature and reality of that future life. Throughout this book we will explore astonishing scientific and medical evidence that strongly suggests that our soul does survive after death as well as the remarkable nature of our future eternal life. In the next chapter we will examine the challenge and meaning of death — one of the greatest mysteries of human existence.

Notes

1. William Blake, "*Auguries of Innocence*," Poems.
2. Thomas Carlyle, rpt. *In Why We May Believe In Life After Death*, Charles E. Jefferson (New York: Houghton Mifflin Co., 1911).

3
The Challenge of Death

Death occurs when the spirit is withdrawn from a human body. From that moment on, both cellular disintegration and chemical decomposition begin to return the body to its natural elements. The pastor declares at a funeral, "From ashes to ashes; from dust to dust." It is fascinating to note that the NASA Ames Research Center in California analyzed the elements found in the human body, and to their surprise they discovered that the Genesis account of man's creation by God from the "dust of the ground" is actually scientifically accurate. Three and a half thousand years ago Moses wrote the following account of man's creation: "And the Lord God formed man of the dust of the ground, and breathed into his nostrils the breath of life; and man became a living being" (Genesis 2:7).

Many scientists naturally dismissed the apparent mythical simplicity of the scriptural account that God utilized "the dust of the ground" to create the complex elements and elaborate molecular structures that make up the awesomely complex human body. However, the NASA scientists discovered that the soil actually contains every one of the elements found in the human body. The NASA scientists concluded, "We are just beginning to learn. The biblical scenario for the creation of life turns out to be not far off the mark." In fact, according to modern science, the biblical account is extraordinarily accurate.

In the book of Genesis Moses recorded the words of God, "For dust thou art, and unto dust shalt thou return" (Genesis 3:19). The great poet, Henry Wadsworth Longfellow, wrote, "Dust thou art, to dust returnest, Was not spoken of the soul." William Shakespeare wrote often about inevitability of death as he did in his play *Macbeth*:

Tomorrow, and tomorrow, and tomorrow,
Creeps in this petty pace from day to day
To the last syllable of recorded time,
And all our yesterdays have lighted fools
The way to dusty death.[1]

In another of his great tragedies Shakespeare described the mystery of death as, "The undiscover'd country from whose bourn No traveller returns." (William Shakespeare: *Hamlet*, Act III, sc. 1, l. 79). While death is universal and therefore common to all of humanity, the personal experience of death is naturally an original, one-of-a-kind experience for each human being. It is no wonder that we look on our own deaths with a certain amount of wonder and fear. When the moment comes for each of us to individually drink its final cup, that experience will be as unique to us as it was to Abel, the first person to ever experience the mystery of death.

The ancient Greek historian, Herodotus, reported in his famous *History of Herodotus* that King Xerxes, the powerful emperor of Persia, wept after watching the review of the awesome military parade in which several million of his soldiers from every part of his vast empire of 127 provinces marched in front of his royal pavilion. Xerxes wept because he realized that not a single one of the millions of men present on the plain that day would still be alive one hundred years later. When the king's uncle, Artabanus, asked him why he was in tears on such a triumphant day, Xerxes responded: "There came upon me a sudden pity, when I thought of the shortness of man's life, and considered that of all this host, so numerous as it is, not one will be alive when a hundred years are gone by."[2]

Our awareness of death affects every other aspect of our life and our relationships. The sixteenth-century Christian poet John Donne wrote, "Death comes equally to us all, and makes us all equal when it comes." Later Donne wrote about how each man's death, whether he is known or unknown to us, profoundly affects every one of us.

> No man is an island, intire of itself;
> every man is piece of the continent, a part of the main;
> if a clod be washed away by the sea, Europe is the less . . .
> Any man's death diminishes me, because I am involved in mankind.
> And therefore never send to know for whom the bell tolls;
> it tolls for thee.[3]

In contrast to the Christian's hopeful expectation of going to heaven following death, many who have no personal faith both fear and fight against death's final approach. The brilliant and troubled Welsh poet, Dylan Thomas, had no confidence of salvation and wrote that we should fight to the last breath against death, "Do not go gentle into that good night, Old age should burn and rave at close of day; Rage, rage against the dying of the light."[4]

The great English historian, Arnold Toynbee, wrote of his uncertainties about death: "Human beings appear to be unique among the fauna inhabiting the biosphere that coats the planet earth in being aware that they themselves and all their living contemporaries are going to die, and that death has already overtaken countless earlier generations. . . . This human awareness of the inevitability of death is accompanied by a concern with death, and Man's concern with death makes him also feel concern about the sequel to death." In another passage Toynbee wrote, "Unlike a physical body, life and consciousness are invisible and impalpable. What, then, has happened to the consciousness that formerly accompanied that person's life? In other words, what has happened to his personality?"[5]

Death is the Last Taboo

The subject of death and eternity is the last real taboo in conversation in our modern western culture, even for Christians. If you doubt that statement, try a small experiment. At the next party you attend, in the middle of a conversation, mention the death of someone you are all familiar with and then ask if anyone present has spent much time thinking about death personally. Watch their reaction. Usually, silence will take over the formerly robust conversation. Although the subject of sex was the great conversational taboo for our Victorian ancestors, the subject of death was often discussed at great length. Today, however, in our modern, "liberated" Western society, the taboo has been reversed. The one subject we studiously avoid is the fact that each of us will someday die and will be faced with a personal eternity of either heaven or hell.

We have more euphemisms and verbal evasions to avoid the topic of death than our grandparents ever did in discussing sex. A well-trained insurance man can spend two hours selling life insurance to you and never once use the words "death" or "die." We say that someone has "passed on," "expired," "breathed his last," "departed," "gone to his eternal rest," or "bought the farm," to name just a few. Our culture hates to say the word "death." Our habit of using euphemisms to avoid speaking directly of death was humorously illustrated in a comedy sketch by an actor on the Monty Python Show some years ago. In the skit a pet-store manager attempted to sell a customer a dead parrot whose feet were nailed to the perch of a birdcage. The customer argued that the parrot was dead. The clerk protested that the parrot was only sleeping:

> This parrot is no more. He has ceased to be. He's expired and gone to meet his maker. He's a stiff. Bereft of life. He rests in peace. If you hadn't nailed him to the perch, he'd be pushing up the daisies. His metabolic processes are now history. He's off the twig. He's kicked the bucket. He's shuffled off this mortal coil, run down the curtain and joined the choir invisible. This is an ex-parrot!

Some of the modern taboos about death were broken by the Swiss-born author Dr. Elizabeth Kubler-Ross in *On Death and Dying*, a book that explores the stages of death and grief that are experienced by both the dying patient and their loved ones. Her book and teaching were enormously helpful to millions of patients, families, and medical staff who had to confront death.[6] While death is a universal phenomenon, and therefore common to all human existence, it is the most solemn experience of our personal life. Death is solemn because it is both certain and uncertain. Death is certain because every one of us must ultimately face our personal death. The Scriptures declare: "It is appointed unto men once to die and after death the judgment" (Hebrews 9:27). Yet death is also uncertain in that not one of us can know with certainty the precise time, the exact place, or the actual circumstances when it shall occur. There is an old expression common to mariners, that each sailor who "went down to the sea in ships" always "sails within four inches of death." Although describing the nearness of death for all seamen, this expression is also true for all of humanity. Every one of us could be only one heartbeat away from death. An anonymous writer once wrote, "This world is but the vestibule of eternity. Every good thought or deed touches a chord that vibrates in heaven." The experience of death is as universal as the experience of birth. Death comes to every human, great or small, rich or poor, and cannot be postponed once God has set our personal appointment with destiny.

Some people may actually look forward to death, believing that it wipes their earthly slates clean of responsibility. William Shakespeare wrote sardonically about the financial finality of death regarding the cancellation of all debts in his play, *The Tempest*. "He that dies pays all his debts."[7] A recent film on organized crime repeated this curious thought when a friend asks a Mafia godfather about the fate of an underworld colleague. The godfather confirmed the death of his colleague when he replied, "Well, let's just say that he doesn't owe nobody any money no more!" While this may be true, only Christ can cleanse our souls from death.

Death first entered the experience of humanity because

of the original sin of our first parents, Adam and Eve. This reality of our inevitable death is confirmed by many Scriptural texts. The Scriptures declare: "For we must needs die, and are as water spilled on the ground, which cannot be gathered up again; neither doth God respect any person: yet doth he devise means, that his banished be not expelled from him" (2 Samuel 14:14). King David wrote of the inevitability of death, "They shall soon be cut down like the grass, and wither as the green herb." (Psalms 37:2). The prophet Isaiah also referred to the universal nature of our death, "All flesh is grass"(Isaiah 40:6).

Only three individuals throughout recorded history ever escaped the finality of physical death — Enoch, Elijah, and Jesus Christ. These three escaped death forever, demonstrating God's power and victory over death and the grave. History records that several individuals in the ancient past experienced death and were supernaturally resuscitated in order to prove Jesus' power over life and death. These individuals include Jarius's daughter and Lazarus; however, they later died a natural death (as verified by the discovery in 1872 of the stone ossuary [coffin] in a burial cave on the edge of the ancient village of Bethany that contained the bones of Lazarus).[8]

Death, the Conqueror, Was Conquered by Christ's Resurrection

The Bible reveals that death is a divine punishment that was decreed to all of humanity following the sinful rebellion of our first parents, Adam and Eve. Therefore, the death of all humans is a spiritual result of the disobedience of humanity to God's revealed will. "Wherefore, as by one man sin entered into the world, and death by sin; and so death passed upon all men, for that all have sinned" (Romans

5:12). But death is not the end; it is only the beginning of a whole new spiritual existence for all those who have died. The English writer Sir Walter Scott wrote, "Is death the last sleep? No, it is the last and final awakening." In the English *Book of Common Prayer* the funeral service contains these words to commemorate the death of a faithful believer: "They rest from their labours."[9] The Church's reference to the "rest" of the body confirms the expectation that our bodies will rise again at the resurrection.

The silence of the grave is frightening to most people. Skeptics point out that the grave has never provided evidence that there is an existence that transcends death. However, both the Old and the New Testament declare the truth of our resurrection from the grave, as we will explore later in this book. The prophet Hosea recorded God's promise: "I will ransom them from the power of the grave; I will redeem them from death" (Hosea 13:14). In fulfilment of numerous Old Testament prophecies, Jesus of Nazareth rose from the dead on the third day after His crucifixion on the cross. The historical evidence of Christ's resurrection, detailed in a later chapter, provides the proof for all humanity that He defeated death personally and triumphed over the grave forever for all those who trust in His promise of salvation. Even prior to His resurrection, Christ proved that He had supernatural power over death and the grave by raising Lazarus and the daughter of Jarius from the dead. Jesus announced this power to His friend Martha after the death of her brother Lazarus: "Jesus said unto her, I am the resurrection, and the life: he that believeth in me, though he were dead, yet shall he live: And whosoever liveth and believeth in me shall never die. Believest thou this?" (John 11:25–26). The resurrection of Christ transformed forever the nature of death for those who place their faith in Him. "The ancients dreaded death: the Christians can only fear dying."[10]

The apostle Paul struggled with our inability to defeat sin and death, but triumphantly declared the victory over these two enemies by Jesus Christ's victorious resurrection.

> O wretched man that I am! who shall deliver me from the body of this death? I thank God through Jesus Christ our Lord. So then with the mind I myself serve the law of God; but with the flesh the law of sin. There is therefore now no condemnation to them which are in Christ Jesus, who walk not after the flesh, but after the Spirit. For the law of the Spirit of life in Christ Jesus hath made me free from the law of sin and death. (Romans 7:24–8:2)

Paul wrote that Jesus Christ had defeated death forever for all those who would place their faith in His salvation: "The last enemy that shall be destroyed is death. . . . O death, where is thy sting? O grave, where is thy victory? The sting of death is sin; and the strength of sin is the law. But thanks be to God, which giveth us the victory through our Lord Jesus Christ" (1 Corinthians 15:26, 55–57). The promise of Jesus Christ regarding eternal life does not exempt His followers from death. Rather, Jesus Christ assures us that faith in Him will ensure that we will triumph over it.

With the fall of Adam and Eve, sin entered into God's perfect Creation. From that moment on until the future moment when Jesus Christ, the Second Adam, will redeem the earth from the curse of sin, our world has travailed under the tragic effects of sin and death. However, the grace and mercy of God refuses to abandon a lost and sinful humanity. Jesus Christ broke the curse of sin and death forever when He triumphed over death and the grave two thousand years ago.

Death is not the end of our life, but only the moment of transcendence to a more spiritual existence that will no longer be restricted by the limits of our present physical and corruptible body. Death opens the door to a more spiritual and lasting experience for our soul. The death of the flower allows its perfume to be released; the death of the chrysalis frees the butterfly from the cocoon to enter into a more beautiful new existence. Similarly, death frees the soul of man from the bonds of flesh to enter into a glorious new spiritual existence in eternity.

Although our ancient forbearers walked in spiritual darkness because they lacked revelation from God about the truths of life, death, and eternity, their ancient art and literature reveal a strong belief in spiritual survival after death. Thirty-five centuries ago a written revelation was given to humanity by God through divinely inspired prophets. From that point on, specific knowledge about our eternal life, heaven, hell, and God's final judgment were described in great detail through these Holy Scriptures, culminating in God's final revelation — Jesus Christ.

During the first century of this era, a small group of religious Jews in Israel called the Sadducees taught that there was no bodily resurrection. They believed that human life is totally material, that the human soul does not survive death. Consequently, the Sadducees often challenged Jesus' teaching because of these beliefs. Conversely, another larger Jewish group, the Pharisees, taught the biblical truth of the resurrection. The significance of the life, death, and resurrection of Jesus of Nazareth is that He claimed for the first time in history that He, as God, had defeated the power of the grave and death forever and had the authority to promise resurrection from death to all those who believed in Him.

Eternity

While eternity is often thought of as something that will only exist after our life on earth is completed, the truth is that eternity exists right now and can be entered into by personal faith in Jesus Christ as your Saviour and Lord. The moment we place our full trust and faith in the salvation offered to us by Jesus Christ through His atoning sacrifice on the cross, we enter into eternal life forever. The medieval English theologian, Thomas Moore, wrote about eternity as follows: "This speck of life in time's great wilderness, This narrow isthmus twixt two boundless seas, The past, the future, two eternities!"[11]

Humans normally perceive time and eternity as opposites, but, to God, who created both, time and eternity are the same. The apostle Peter wrote, "But, beloved, be not ignorant of this one thing, that one day is with the Lord as a thousand years, and a thousand years as one day" (2 Peter 3:8). However, Christians who place their trust and faith in Jesus Christ partake of both time and eternity from the moment of salvation. Jesus declared, "My sheep hear my voice, and I know them, and they follow me: And I give unto them eternal life; and they shall never perish, neither shall any man pluck them out of my hand" (John 10:27–28). Those who follow Christ already possess eternal life, and at death shall be united with God throughout eternity. However, even on this earth, believers are in the blessed presence of God. As the apostle Paul wrote, "Now if we be dead with Christ, we believe that we shall also live with him: Knowing that Christ being raised from the dead dieth no more; death hath no more dominion over him" (Romans 6:8–9).

Many aging Christians experience the sadness that comes from attending more and more funerals of their great friends and relatives who have passed away before them. Sometimes it must seem as if they will be the last of their once numerous group of friends who still lives on. However, they can comfort themselves with the thoughts of a fellow Christian, John Keble, who wrote,

Tis sweet, as year by year we lose
Friends out of sight, in faith to muse
How grows in Paradise our store.[12]

Our Appointment with Death

At some point in time, death approaches each human with the sobering announcement that our time on earth is through. The Scriptures record one such appointment: "In those days was Hezekiah sick unto death. And the prophet Isaiah the son of Amoz came to him, and said unto him, Thus saith the Lord, Set thine house in order; for thou shalt die, and not live" (2 Kings 20:1). Just as God instructed the prophet Isaiah to warn the king of Judah that his death was at hand, He may send us intimations when our appointment with destiny approaches. Perhaps He does this as a warning, giving some people one last chance, as in the following story:

> There was once a German nobleman who led a foolish and dissapated life; drinking, gambling and neglecting his vassals, his family and his affairs. He had a dream, one night, which vividly impressed him. He saw a figure, looking at him with serious face, and pointing to a dial, where the hands marked the hour of four. The figure looked at him sadly, and said these words: "After four!" and disappeared.

The nobleman awoke in great terror, and thought that vision foreboded his speedy death. What could it mean? It must mean that he was to die after four days, so he determined to "set his house in order." He sent for the priest, confessed his sins and received absolution. He sent for his family, and begged their forgiveness for his offences against them. He sent for his man of business, and arranged his affairs as well as he could. He then waited for death. The four days passed, and he did not die. He then thought that perhaps the vision meant that he was to die after four weeks. He had a longer time for preparation; so he devoted these four weeks to making atonement for all the evil he had done in the world, and doing all the good he could. The four weeks passed, and he was still alive. Then he thought it meant four months, and so he spent these four months in a more thorough repentance; he did all the good he could in that time on his estates; he found out all the poor and the sufferers, and helped them. The four months passed, and he did not die. Then he said, "It is plain that the vision meant "four years." So during that four years, he gave all his thoughts and time to others; did all he could for his neighbors, his vassals, the poor; and also took useful and honorable part in public affairs. At the end of four years, instead of dying, he was chosen Emperor of Germany, and became one of the best emperors that ever was elected. The expectation of death had taught him how to live. It was natural that it should do so.[13]

Deathbed Conversions

It is possible, though rare, that a man or woman may repent of their sinful life at the very moment he or she faces death. Jesus proclaimed to the repentant thief dying on the cross, "Today you will be with me in Paradise." However, while we cannot deny the possibility of genuine deathbed conversions, our knowledge of human nature and personal experience suggests that such deathbed conversions are quite rare. While many who reject the claims of Christ today may vainly hope that they will have a final opportunity to repent of their sins on their deathbed, the reality of most deaths is that there is often little or no warning. Those who plan to repent on their deathbed are risking their very souls. If you have ever had the experience of visiting someone who is dying, you know that deathbeds may involve great pain, heavy medication, disconnected thoughts, and intrusive medical procedures. This is a very unlikely place for a sober review of your life and a sincere repentance before your final and irrevocable loss of consciousness.

> To speak of death as a sleep is an image common to all languages and nations. Thereby the reality of death is not denied, but only the fact implicitly assumed, that death will be followed by a resurrection, as sleep is by an awakening. (Archbishop Trench)

Final Words Before Death

A dying person's last words are accepted in many societies as having the same legal importance of a written last will and testament, in recognition of the fact that a person is unlikely to speak falsely in their dying moments. Common sense and human experience have shown that men will seldom consciously lie when they know they are facing the prospect of eternity and their final appointment to meet God as their judge.

The writer Thomas à Kempis spoke of the need to prepare now for that final moment of life. "Strive now so to live that you may be able in the hour of death to rejoice rather than to fear. Learn now to die to the world that you may then begin to live with Christ."[14]

In 1728, the great writer and statesman Benjamin Franklin ordered that the following epitaph be written on his gravestone in recognition of his strong hope of the resurrection: "The body of B. Franklin Printer (Like the Cover of an Old Book, Its Contents torn out And stript of its Lettering & Gilding) Lies here, food for Worms. But the work shall not be lost: For it will, (as he believ'd) appear once more, In a new and more elegant Edition Revised and corrected, By the Author." Henry Alford, the Christian writer of the hymn *Ten Thousand Times Ten Thousand* requested that the following epitaph be engraved on his tombstone in Canterbury, England. It reflected his confident faith that the grave was but a temporary stop along our journey towards the New Jerusalem. The epitaph read: "The inn of a pilgrim journeying to Jerusalem."

The Dying Words of Unbelievers

Men often express bravado and contempt of death when all is well in their life, saying, "Eat, drink and be merry, for tomorrow we die!" However, when death stands at the door, their words often change to reflect utter terror in view of the bankruptcy of their vain philosophies. In the light of the knowledge that dying words reflect men's truest thoughts, consider some of the last testaments of some famous people who knew they were dying without Christ.

Queen Elizabeth I was one of England's greatest

monarchs. She created a powerful British empire that dominated Europe for several centuries. However, as she lay dying, the Queen realized that she had not prepared as well for her death as she had prepared herself to run the government of her great and growing empire. As she felt her last moments fleeting away, she faced her approaching death and plaintively asked, "All my possessions for a moment of time." However, when our final hour comes, no power on earth can restrain the approach of the angel of death.

Thomas Paine, one of the greatest infidels and enemies of Christianity, wrote a famous anti-Christian book entitled *The Age of Reason*. However, Paine provided a sobering illustration of the last conscious moments of one who dies in agony apart from faith in Christ. According to those who witnessed his deathbed scene, Thomas Paine died without any peace. "He would call out during his paroxysms of distress, 'O Lord, help me! God, help me! Jesus Christ, help me!' repeating the same expressions without the least variations, in a tone that would alarm the house. 'I would give worlds if I had them,' he cried, 'that *The Age of Reason* had never been published.'"[15] Another great enemy of Christ, the fifteenth-century English philosopher Thomas Hobbes, spent his adult life arguing that Christianity was logically insupportable. However, his confidence abandoned him as he lay on his deathbed: "I am taking a fearful leap in the dark!"

The Dying Words of Believers

Those who face death knowing their place in the heart of God can face it with confidence. In contrast to the words of those famous atheists who died in fear, there are multitudes of examples of the dying words of Christians that illustrate the tremendous gulf separating the spiritual prospects and attitudes of believers from those who have never known the experience of Jesus Christ in their lives. The Lord warned His disciples about the persecution that would afflict them wherever they preached the Gospel. There is a natural hatred of divine truth that rises within the heart of those who reject God's law. They form a deep contempt for the holy lives and the selfless love of followers of Christ.

In the countries that persecuted them, Christians have been the most law-abiding, tax-paying, and loyal of citizens. They actually pray for the good of their persecutors, yet the evil leaders of this world are sometimes driven by their satanic hatred to persecute the Church because they view the existence of a dynamic Christianity as a reproach against their personal sins and widespread corruption. However, the blood of the Christian martyrs ultimately has inspired whole generations to abandon the spiritually bankrupt philosophies of paganism to follow Jesus Christ. During the last few centuries, the Christians in North America have experienced freedom from the horrors of persecution; however, throughout most of the rest of the world, our faithful Christian brothers and sisters are called upon daily to prove their faith with their life's blood. Over one hundred thousand Christians a year are killed as martyrs. In the south of Sudan in East Africa, Moslem army units have continually raided Christian villages for the last two decades. Hundreds of Christian Sudanese men have been crucified, and their wives and children have been sold as slaves in North Africa and Saudi Arabia. As the apostle Paul warned, "We are persecuted on every side, yet not forsaken; cast down, but not destroyed" (2 Corinthians 4:8–9). Consider the dying words in the following accounts that testify to the faith of those who loved Jesus Christ, even at the cost of their lives. Stephen was one of the first seventy deacons of the first-century Jerusalem church. He became the first martyr of the new Christian faith when he was stoned to death in the early days of the Christian Church. Stephen gave eloquent witness to his faith in Jesus to those preparing to stone him. Rather than appeal for mercy or respond by cursing his oppressors, Stephen looked up steadfastly towards his home in heaven and said, "Behold, I see the heavens opened, and the Son of man standing on the right hand of God. Then they cried out with a loud voice, and stopped their ears, and ran upon him with one accord, And cast him out of the city, and stoned him: and the witnesses laid down their clothes at a young man's feet, whose name was Saul. And they stoned Stephen, calling upon God, and saying, Lord Jesus, receive my spirit" (Acts 7:55–59).

The English king, Charles I, awaited his execution on the scaffold in the courtyard of the Tower of London. As he knelt to place his neck on the block, he declared his unshakable faith in Christ and the final promise of resurrection: "I go from a corruptible to an incorruptible crown, where no disturbance can have place." The king of France, King Louis, was called Saint Louis because of his unusual dedication to Jesus Christ. His holy life was exceedingly rare among medieval monarchs. As he was dying, the king declared, "O Lord, I will go into thy house, I will offer my prayer in thine holy temple, and will glorify thy name."

The Protestant Reformation led to a transformation of Christianity in Europe. For the first time in a thousand years, Christian laymen began to study the Scriptures in their own languages. As these men and women studied the Bible, they quickly rediscovered the foundational truths of Christianity based on justification by faith. The Reformation produced a great number of martyrs in Europe who died rather than deny their faith in Jesus Christ. The great reformer of Eastern

Europe, Jerome of Prague, when led to the stake to be burned for his unshakable faith in Jesus Christ and the Word of God, announced, "This soul in flames I offer, Christ, to thee." When another reformer, John Huss, faced his own martyrdom for his unflinching defense of the Christian faith based on the truth of the Holy Scriptures, he declared, "I take God to witness, I preached none but his own pure doctrines, and what I taught I am ready to seal with my blood." Archbishop Cranmer bore the flames of his martyrdom in full confidence of his Lord. Facing imminent death, Cranmer declared, as did St. Stephen centuries earlier, "Lord Jesus, receive my spirit."

Martin Luther became the father of the Protestant Reformation in A.D. 1520. After years of agonizing works, doubt, spiritual suffering, and deep longings for true forgiveness of his sins, Luther finally discovered the liberating truth of salvation in the words of the Holy Scriptures: "The just shall live by faith" (Habakkuk 2:4, Galatians 3:11). This radical truth of personal salvation through faith in Christ was the fundamental teaching of both the Old and New Testaments. The biblical doctrine of justification by faith in Jesus Christ's atoning work on the cross, as opposed to the failed doctrine of works, became the ultimate spiritual rallying cry of the Protestant Reformation, a spiritual revolution that released hundreds of millions from the shackles of a dead medieval religion. When Luther approached his own death he said, "Thou hast redeemed me, O Lord God of truth. I will die steadfast, clinging to Christ and to the doctrine I have so constantly preached."

The Italian reformer, Jerome Savonarola, who faced martyrdom for his unflinching faith in Christ, faced his executioners with these words, "My Lord died for my sins; shall not I gladly give this poor life for him?" As death approached Lord Francis Bacon, one of the most brilliant scientists of his age, he declared his personal faith in Christ, "Thy creatures, O Lord, have been my books, but thy Holy Scriptures much more. I have sought thee in the courts, fields and gardens; but I have found thee, O God, in thy sanctuary, thy temples." Even John Calvin, the reformer from Switzerland, faced death with these words: "Lord, thou bruisest me, but it is enough for me to know that it is thou."

One of the most famous ladies in English history was Anne Boleyn who rose from obscurity to become the royal wife of the notorious King Henry VIII. When King Henry desired a new wife, he falsely accused her of treason to justify her execution. As she faced her death on the scaffold, Anne Boleyn confessed her unshakable faith in Christ's promise of heaven and addressed her executioner: "Commend me to the King, and tell him he is constant in his course of advancing me. From a private gentlewoman he made me a marquisse; and from a marquisse, a queen; and now he hath left no higher degree of earthly honor, he hath made me a martyr."[16]

Reverend Cotton Mather was a great American teacher of the Word of God and a well-known preacher in the 1700s. As he lay dying he said, "Is this dying? Is this all? O, I can bear this! I can bear it! I can bear it!" The great European composer, Ludwig van Beethoven, who has produced some of the greatest music ever recorded, even though he was deaf, confidently announced to those at his deathbed, "I shall hear in heaven." General George Washington, the first president of the United States, was a strong Christian believer with a powerful faith in his Saviour. When he was dying, Washington announced, "It is well." At the funeral of the great American preacher Dr. Charles H. Spurgeon, the following words were sung based on Sarah Doudney's *The Christian's Good-night*: "Sleep on, beloved, sleep, and take thy rest; Lay down thy head upon thy Savior's breast. We love thee well, but Jesus loved thee best — Good-night! Good-night! Good-night!"

Mourning for the Dead

The Scriptures reveal numerous examples of people who mourned for their deceased loved ones. Even our Lord Jesus Christ Himself wept when He approached the town of Bethany knowing that His beloved friend Lazarus was now dead. Though Christ knew in His supernatural foreknowledge that He would revive Lazarus to live again for a time in this world, as a living witness to Christ's own resurrection from the grave, He still wept when He contemplated the loss of the friendship and love that Lazarus' sisters experienced. The Old Testament reveals the profound love of the patriarch Abraham for his beloved wife, Sarah, when she finally surrendered to death. The Scriptures tell us that Joseph, the acclaimed prince of Egypt, wept profoundly for his father Jacob for seven days, and the children of Israel wept and mourned for thirty days when their beloved leader Moses died just before they entered the Promised Land. Although King David wrote confidently about the truth of our final resurrection, he was overcome with grief and mourned deeply for the loss of King Saul and his son, Jonathan.

While the mourning of Jesus and other saints obviously reveals that this is a normal response to the loss of a loved one, those who are Christians who mourn for departed saints can be comforted with the knowledge that we weep for ourselves and our loss of companionship, but can rejoice in the knowledge that our departed loved one is now safely and joyfully in Heaven with Jesus and the other saints forever.

Funeral Customs of the Ancients

While some scholars have suggested that the Old Testament taught the doctrine of resurrection of the dead, a careful examination of the Scriptures reveals that the truth of our bodily resurrection was taught from Genesis to Malachi. The Jewish people, beginning with Abraham, carefully buried the body of loved ones in the anticipation that they would rise again in the last days. The pagan practices of either cremation or of abandoning the body above the ground were disturbing to the Jews. In the oldest books of the Bible, we find positive expressions concerning our ultimate bodily resurrection from the dead. For example, in Genesis, Moses wrote, "Then Abraham gave up the ghost, and died in a good old age, an old man, and full of years; and was gathered to his people" (Genesis 25:8). Later we find the following statement about his son Isaac's burial. "And Isaac gave up the ghost, and died, and was gathered unto his people, being old and full of days: and his sons Esau and Jacob buried him" (Genesis 35:29). The common biblical expression of being "gathered unto his people" is one of many biblical statements that confirms the belief that our spirits continue to exist consciously and will be gathered together with other believers.

The Jews called their burial ground "Beth-haim," meaning, "the house of the living." This name acknowledges their fundamental belief that their bodies will rise in the last days to be "gathered to their fathers." The Greek name for a burial ground or graveyard is *coemeterian,* meaning, "sleeping place." This term was used by the early Christians to reflect the fact that only our bodies rest in the ground, while our spirits rise to heaven to rejoice consciously in the presence of Jesus Christ until the day of our glorious resurrection.

Many scholars believe that the book of Job is the most ancient book in the Bible. It is fascinating, therefore, that the book of Job clearly teaches the doctrine of bodily resurrection in the last days. When he contemplated his own death, Job wrote, "For I know that my redeemer liveth, and that he shall stand at the latter day upon the earth: And though after my skin worms destroy this body, yet in my flesh shall I see God: Whom I shall see for myself, and mine eyes shall behold, and not another; though my reins be consumed within me" (Job 19:25–27). Note the strength of language used by Job to confirm that he will personally survive in his resurrected flesh to see God. Despite the obvious impending destruction of his physical body, Job assures us that "mine eyes shall behold, and not another; though my reins be consumed within me."

The pagan nations that surrounded Israel normally engaged in the cremation of the body, usually in anticipation of either annihilation of the soul or reincarnation of individuals in future bodies. Cremation prefigured the rebirth of the entity into another future body, symbolized by the mythical Phoenix bird rising from the ashes of the fire. However, the Bible's rejection of the pagan doctrine of reincarnation is absolute. The writer of the book of Hebrews (probably Paul) said, "And as it is appointed unto men once to die, but after this the judgment" (Hebrews 9:27). A careful study of the totality of the Scripture's teaching about life and death confirms that the Bible firmly rejects the doctrine of reincarnation.

It is significant that Jesus of Nazareth was buried in a tomb, as were all of the disciples in the Christian Church. For example, according to Acts 5: 1–10, Ananias and Sapphira were immediately buried following their death. Recent archeological discoveries of stone coffins containing the remains of Jewish-Christian believers, including Mary, Martha, and Lazarus in Bethany, together with individuals such as Alexander, the son of Simeon of Cyrene who carried the Cross of Christ confirm the popularity and acceptance of burial in the ground or in caves. The universal burial practices of both the early Church as well as the customs of Christians and the Jewish synagogues in every nation for the last two thousand years demonstrate respectful treatment of the human body and its careful burial in the ground. These Jewish and Christian practices are performed with the conscious expectation of the coming Day of Judgment, when the bodies of the saints will be resurrected into new spiritual and immortal bodies that will be fit for eternal life in both heaven and earth.

The ultimate triumph of Jesus Christ over death and the grave forever is announced by the prophet John in his book of Revelation. John declared, "Blessed are the dead which die in the Lord from henceforth: Yea, saith the Spirit, that they may rest from their labours; and their works do follow them" (Revelation 14:13).

Notes

1. William Shakespeare, *Macbeth* (Chicago: The University of Chicago, 1982).
2. J. H. Potts, *Golden Dawn* (Philadelphia: P. W. Ziegler & Co., 1880).
3. John Donne, *Devotions Upon Emergent Occasions*.
4. Dylan Thomas, *Do Not Go Gentle Into That Good Night*.
5. Arnold Toynbee, *Life After Death* (London: Weidenfeld and Nicolson, 1976).
6. Elizabeth Kubler-Ross, *On Death and Dying* (New York: Macmillan, 1971).
7. William Shakespeare, *The Tempest* (Chicago: The University of Chicago, 1982).
8. Charles Claremont-Gannueau, *Palestine Exploration Fund Report* 1873-1874.
9. "Service for the Burial of the Dead," *Book of Common Prayer*.
10. William Augustus and Julius Charles Hare, *Guesses at Truth*.
11. Thomas Moore, *Lala Rookh, The Veiled Prophet of Khorassan*.
12. John Keble, *Burial of the Dead*.
13. J. H. Potts, *Golden Dawn* (Philadelphia: P. W. Ziegler & Co., 1880).
14. Thomas à Kempis, *Imitation of Christ*.
15. Oswald J. Smith, *The Battle for Truth* (London: Marshall, Morgan & Scott, 1962) 38.
16. J. H. Potts, *Golden Dawn* (Philadelphia: P. W. Ziegler & Co., 1880).

4

Near Death Experiences

During the last few decades there has been an increasing number of reports from doctors, nurses, and scientists about patients who had clinically died, but were later revived, who claim have had profound spiritual experiences during their crises. These remarkable events are now called *near death experiences* (NDE). Naturally, the possibility that these reports provide scientific evidence of the survival of the human soul after death is fascinating to many people. Extraordinary advances in medical techniques, sophisticated medications, and modern trauma technology have greatly increased the chance that someone may be resuscitated. However, the topic of near death experiences is very controversial. As you review the information in this chapter you will see that virtually every aspect of this subject is beset with controversy. The most controversial aspect of the near death experience for most people is the lack of independent and scientifically verified evidence to support the claims of its proponents. For those Christians who place their faith in the teaching of the Scriptures, the major problem with most of the popular books on NDEs is that they suggest that everyone goes to Heaven regardless of their behavior or beliefs. This suggestion completely contradicts our natural sense of justice and the teachings of the Bible about the need for repentance and faith in Jesus Christ.

Reports of Near Death Experiences

People who experience NDEs often assert that they felt their spirit lift out of their body. Once freed from their body, they sometimes viewed their body lying on the bed from a position above. Some then experienced a sensation of traveling to another place. Often they reported seeing a powerful white light at the end of a long tunnel and feeling a sense of overwhelming unconditional love. Some claim to have encountered a spiritual being of light who communicates with them. Often, Christians who claim to remember a near death experience have said that they met Jesus Christ. Those who meet a spiritual being sometimes say they were told, often without audible words, that they must return to their body because they still had unfinished business to complete. However, one of the most controversial claims in many of the recent best-selling books about the near death experience is that some participants state that the spiritual being told them that their personal beliefs, their religion, or their unrepented evil deeds had no effect on their future spiritual state. Significantly, these reports differ substantially from those of Christians. Several researchers have noted that generally Christians do not recount these New Age elements in their NDEs.[1]

Perhaps the earliest recorded near death experience in history is found in the writings of the Greek philosopher Plato. He wrote about a soldier who was thought to have died but recovered consciousness when his supposedly dead body was placed on a funeral pyre for burning. This soldier claimed to have had an NDE.[2] Other historical references to near death experiences are found in ancient writings, including Buddhist texts in China dating back to at least four centuries prior to the birth of Christ.

Over a century ago, in the 1890s, the first significant scientific study about these unusual experiences was published in Switzerland. Albert Heim, a Swiss mountain climber, fell off a cliff but miraculously survived when he landed on soft snow. During his near death experience, Heim reported that time appeared to slow down. All fear of death vanished, and there was a brilliant explosion of colors and music and a film-like review of the important events of his life from his days as a child until the present. Although there was little attention paid to this report, an English translation of this study by Dr. Russell Noyes at the University of Iowa in the 1970s revived public and academic awareness of this unusual medical and spiritual experience.

Since then there has been a veritable explosion of books, articles, and television documentaries that explore this extraordinary and provocative medical phenomenon. The first major book to bring this NDE phenomenon to the masses was best-seller *Life After Life*, written by Dr. Raymond A. Moody Jr., in 1975. Although Dr. Moody, a physician and writer, initially rejected NDEs, he did complete the first serious study of this phenomenon. He was quite skeptical, but after hearing a story from another psychiatrist, George Ritchie, who professed to have had an NDE while dying from pneumonia as a soldier during World War II, Moody continued his research. After interviewing fifty additional patients, he was finally convinced that NDEs pointed inexorably to the fact that our spirit somehow continues to live after our physical death.[3] Dr. Moody's continued study of NDEs resulted in two additional books in the following decades.

Dr. Moody, in *Life After Life*, said, "Near death experiences represent a novel phenomenon for which we have to devise new modes of explanation and interpretation. If near-death experiences are real, they have very profound implications for our lives; we can't fully understand this life until we catch a glimpse of what lies beyond."[4] His book examined many similar NDEs recounted by a large number of hospital patients who shared their experiences with him. Evidence from hospitals and doctors throughout the world confirmed that millions of individuals from every tribe, nation, religion, and language claim to have had NDEs. Naturally, Moody's book met with a good deal of natural skepticism from doctors, psychiatrists, and scientists. One of the problems with his study was that it had no real scientific controls. He did not document the medical procedures or the physical condition of the patients during their crises. Furthermore, the accounts were often given to Moody years or decades after the patients' experiences, raising the possibility that they could have been influenced by memory lapses or false recollections caused by hearing lectures on NDEs.[5]

Dr. Melvin Morse, a pediatrician who has encountered NDEs in a number of small children under his care, wrote his first book on the subject, entitled *Closer to the Light*, in 1990. Morse raised serious questions about the nature of the reported NDEs detailed by other researchers, including

Dr. Moody. Interestingly, Dr. Morse notes that Dr. Moody "readily acknowledges asking loaded questions" in his interviews with patients. Dr. Morse adds that Dr. Raymond Moody's research was, in fact, "based on subjects who often approached Dr. Moody after lectures, [and that] no systematic interview format was involved, and no review of medical records or psychiatric or medical history was done."

The psychologist Dr. Kenneth Ring completed a more balanced scientific study involving 102 patients. These individuals confirmed virtually all of the details recounted by Dr. Moody. However, Dr. Morse again questioned the scientific objectivity of this research. Dr. Morse criticized Ring's book, *Life at Death.* He said, "The book is filled with impressive statistics based on a biased subject sample and poor data collection techniques."

More recently, a women named Betty Eadie wrote an extremely popular book about this phenomenon entitled *Embraced By The Light*. It was on the *New York Times* best-seller list for many months and has sold millions of copies. Her book is curious in that it is written almost twenty years after her reported NDE. Despite requests by other researchers, she is alleged to have refused access to the medical files that detail her condition. Her book postulates that everyone is perfect and that all humans will go to Heaven regardless of their behavior or beliefs. Although many readers would never realize it, Betty Eadie's book presents numerous Mormon beliefs. These include such falsehoods as the claim that God is simply a man like ourselves, and that we ourselves can become gods. Her book suggests that every religion is equally valid and that every one of us in the end will be saved. In addition, the book denies the consequences of sin and rejects the biblical truth that every human will ultimately be judged by God.

A skeptical physician, Dr. Michael Sabom, studied the NDE phenomenon for five years. He interviewed 116 patients who had undergone death-like experiences. As the staff physician at the Atlanta Veterans Administration Hospital, Sabom was in a unique position to carefully examine these patients' medical records to verify their experiences. Seventy-one of these patients reported that they had had an NDE. Many experienced an overwhelming sense of love and peace and claimed to have met loved ones who had died earlier. Some experienced traveling through a tunnel towards a light, and a few claimed they met Christ. Interestingly, 32 of the 71 patients experienced the sensation of their consciousness lifting above their bodies, as they watched the medical procedures that were used to resuscitate them. When these 32 patients were asked to describe what they observed while they were unconscious, 26 of them correctly described the medical details in general terms. However, six of the patients provided extremely detailed descriptions of the step-by-step resuscitation procedures that occurred while they were totally unconscious.

Dr. Sabom recorded that one patient described with incredible accuracy how, while unconscious, he was able to observe the nurses using the electric paddles of the defibrillator to shock his heart. He expressed great surprise that his body "leapt" almost a foot off the operating table when his body was shocked. People who have not personally observed this medical procedure would never guess that the body would react so violently to the shock because television and movies can never accurately depict this scene. Another patient described in great detail every stage of his open-heart operation, including the placement of a needle into his heart to remove air and the careful stitching of the wound, beginning from the inside heart tissue and continuing to the chest muscles. Another one of these six patients was face down and unconscious throughout a back lumbar disk operation. However, she correctly described that the chief neurosurgeron of the hospital, whom she hadn't seen until after the operation, actually performed the surgery. She could not have known this normally because she was unconscious under anesthesia. Dr. Sabom became convinced by this evidence that the NDE was a genuine phenomenon.[6]

Most NDEs tend to occur following a heart attack, serious illness, major surgery, suicide attempt, or severe trauma due to an accident. Surprisingly, some people have experienced a very similar phenomenon without undergoing a major medical crisis. The number of reported cases is now so overwhelming that even skeptics and critics have gradually abandoned the attempt to deny them. One study in Australia, in 1989, suggested that as many as 10 percent of those adults surveyed indicated that they had experienced at least a few of the basic elements that normally accompany an NDE. The critics now generally accept them as genuine experiences, but tend to deny that this suggests that our spirit somehow survives the death of our body. Rather, the critics tend to suggest other factors, such as hallucination, medication, or previously held religious expectations, as the true cause of the remembered experience.

Remarkable claims have been made that suggest that some who undergo this experience are still conscious of events even when the monitors indicate no brain or heart activity. Some unconscious, near-death patients remember conversations held in adjoining rooms, or other events occurring outside the range of their sense organs. There are no clear medical or scientific explanations for these experiences.[7] During the last few decades, detailed research on NDEs has been conducted at the University of Connecticut's International Association for Near-Death Studies (IANDS). This research has continuously promoted a view of the afterlife that is very anti-biblical. Although IANDS is now a major source of published near death experiences, its articles are generally not reviewed by other scientists, nor does its research appear in regular scientific or medical literature.

The *Journal for Near-Death Studies* now explores most of the evidence that continues to accumulate from around the world about this phenomenon. The growing interest in near death experiences has expanded to the point that there are now hundreds of Internet web sites that share information, testimonies, and research on this subject. In fact, the popular Internet online bookstore, Amazon.com, currently offers over ninety different books that explore the topic. The International Association for Near-Death Studies shares its latest research and accounts through its web site: http://www.iands.org/index.html.

Growing Awareness of the Near Death Experience

The growing public awareness about this medical phenomenon was enhanced and influenced by the 1990s movie *Fearless,* starring actor Jeff Bridges. This movie explored the profound personality changes that some passengers experienced after having near death experiences following a terrible plane crash.

A 1982 study by the Gallup Poll organization found that an astonishing five percent of the adults surveyed admitted to personally having had a near death experience at some point in their life. According to the 1994 survey, approximately twelve million Americans claim to have had an NDE. A more recent survey in 1996 by *USA Today* calculated that thirteen million citizens have had near death experiences.[8] However, other researchers disagree, reporting that less than one percent of those who experienced near death medical emergencies — where monitored life signs ceased — and then returned to normal consciousness reported having an NDE.[9]

Personal Impact

Near death experiences can cause profound spiritual, emotional, and intellectual changes. Many individuals and their families report that the NDE produced significant personality changes. This tends to suggest that the experience is genuine. These reports imply that the NDE is not simply a hallucination produced by the traumatic experience of dying, or a side effect of a particular drug administered during a medical crisis.

On February 1, 2000, Pam Barrett, the leader of the New Democratic Party in Alberta, Canada, was undergoing anesthesia in her dentist's office. Suddenly she had a violent allergic reaction to the anesthetic, and her breathing stopped. Within moments she knew she was dying, but she felt an enormous sense of peace as she perceived that there was a true spiritual reality that far surpassed anything she had ever believed. Barrett said, "I was on the other side long enough to feel the peace of God. . . . I was without challenge or pain and, most important, without fear. When I was dead, all I knew was that this [was] the ultimate happiness." A few hours later, while in the hospital, she "died" a second time and felt her consciousness leaving her body. She claims to have experienced an overwhelming sense of being surrounded by light and total comfort. Remarkably, though she was a nonpracticing Catholic who previously rejected the possibility of immortality, this experience so transformed her that she immediately called her political office within two hours of her first NDE to announce that she was resigning her leadership role and leaving politics forever. She now admits, "Spiritual matters hadn't had any part in my life before, but they're a big part of it now."[10]

Reports About the After Effects

Continuing research on individuals who have undergone a near death experience has revealed a remarkable number of similar changes in the lives of people following their NDEs. This is confirmed by such researchers as C. Sutherland, Kenneth Ring, and P. M. H. Atwater. These common elements appear as personality changes or belief changes, and can include the following:

1) A belief in life after death
2) An almost total lack of fear of death
3) A development of a deep interest in their personal spiritual progress
4) A more positive view about themselves and of those around them
5) A greater awareness and sense of spiritual purpose to their life
6) A desire for solitude and thoughtfulness
7) An increased concern for personal health and learning
8) The cessation of the use of drugs, tobacco, and a reduced use of alcohol
9) A career change toward a job involved with helping people
10) A decreased interest in the news[11]

In *Beyond The Light,* Atwater reports that only one of her 3000 subjects could stand listening to rock music after their NDE.[12] Anyone who has ever managed employees or raised children knows how very difficult it is to change people's character or behavior patterns. Therefore, these reported changes suggest that these NDEs were genuine.

However, Dr. Kenneth Ring also noted in his book *Heading Toward Omega* that numerous people undergo depression, divorce, and a certain degree of psychological alienation from normal human relationships and events after an NDE.[13]

Possible Medical Explanations

Many doctors and researchers reject the claims of those who state there is a spiritual element to the near death experience. These doctors point to the fact that a significant loss of blood flow to the brain can bring about changes in our consciousness. For example, Dr. Angela Genge, a neurologist at the Montreal Neurological Institute, claims that changes in the blood supply to the brain during a medical crisis can cause tunnel vision and other phenomena similar to what is reported during an NDE. Dr. Genge suggests that some of the effects of an NDE can be explained by neurological damage caused by this loss of blood. However, she admits that while a few of the elements of the near death experience can be explained by neurological changes in the brain, many of the NDE elements cannot be explained medically.[14]

One of the problems with the proposed physiological explanations, such as the lack of sufficient oxygen to the brain due to reduced blood flow, is that oxygen starvation normally produces massive confusion in the patient's mind and is followed by unconsciousness. However, patients are able to report their NDE and describe feeling an unusual calmness. Other possible explanations include hallucinations caused by medications. Yet many of those who undergo NDEs had no exposure to drugs. Additionally, those patients who describe their NDEs clearly reject the thought that they have experienced hallucinations. The reported character and lifestyle changes associated with NDEs are not associated with hallucinations. Some have suggested that high levels of carbon dioxide in the blood might produce sensory images similar to those reported with the NDE. However, Dr. Sabom examined the medical operation records of one NDE patient whose blood gas levels were constantly measured during his operation. The blood gas readings revealed that the patient actually had high levels of oxygen and a lower than normal level of carbon dioxide. Therefore, high carbon dioxide levels in the bloodstream are an unlikely reason for the experience.

Other skeptics have suggested the possibility that the brain may have produced large amounts of endorphins, accounting for the NDE. Endorphins are naturally occurring brain chemicals that minimize pain. Dr. Sabom dismisses this possibility because the NDE eliminates pain only during the few minutes of the actual experience; the pain returns instantly when the consciousness returns to the body. High endorphin levels remain in the bloodstream for many hours and would provide pain relief for a long period of time.

Serious Reservations About the Near Death Experience

Since the release of the popular books in the 1970s, many Christian pastors as well as Christian lay people have raised serious concerns over the spiritual implications of some of the claims of the NDE researchers. When we examine the NDE research completed by Dr. Raymond Moody and Dr.

Melvin Morse we find that much of their reported research lacks any serious scientific controls. For example, most of the evidence is volunteered by those participants who have shared their NDE after previously reading about other people's experiences. This self-selection creates serious problems with the credibility of the data. At the least, it is likely that those who remembered pleasant elements of the NDE would be far more likely to choose to be interviewed and quoted in a book on the subject than those who had a negative experience. In addition, the lack of detailed medical evidence about the participants makes it very difficult to evaluate whether or not they were ever clinically dead.

Another criticism questions the use of leading questions some researchers employ to interview claimants. Examples from the Greyson Near Death Experience Validity Scale, the actual questionnaire used by Dr. B. Greyson to elicit data about the memories of the NDE, reveals the unscientific and suggestive nature of the questions used:[15]

"Did scenes from your past come back to you?"

"Did you have a feeling of peace or pleasantness?"

"Did you have a feeling of joy?"

"Did you see or feel surrounded by a brilliant light?"

"Did scenes from the future come to you?"

"Did you feel separated from your physical body?"

"Did you seem to encounter a mystical being or presence?"

"Did you see deceased spirits or religious figures?"

Obviously, these extremely leading questions can suggest to the NDE claimant the type of answer the researcher is looking for.

Another problem is that there have been over a dozen bestselling books, numerous magazine articles, and many television documentaries that have explored this subject since Dr. Moody's *Life After Life*. As a result of the incredible publicity given this fascinating phenomenon in the last quarter century, most people have heard the curious stories about tunnels, bright lights, strange spiritual beings, and the sense of physical detachment from the body. Therefore, it is very likely that anyone interviewed by a researcher concerning a personal near death experience would be influenced by their memories and expectations about what "normally" occurs during an NDE. Surprisingly, considering that a number of these best-selling authors are medical doctors, very little medical research has been conducted on the patients to confirm what actually happened to them medically. One researcher, cardiologist Dr. F. Schoonmaker, who collected information on NDEs for eighteen years from patients who underwent medical crises in a Denver hospital, admitted that many of the patients initially claimed that they had no memory whatsoever of the experience. Schoonmaker admitted that many of the persons quoted in his study could remember their NDE "only after repeated invitations and reassurances."[16]

It is obvious to anyone who examines these popular best-selling books that many people are very attracted to the claim that this phenomenon "proves" that no one needs fear that they will go to Hell after death. The attractive, loving, and enjoyable spiritual future that is promised to everyone, regardless of their beliefs or sinful deeds, is naturally considered wonderful news to those who would like to escape the biblical teaching about the danger of Hell. However, this proclamation of universal salvation by the majority of NDE books stands in total contradiction to the teaching of Jesus Christ in the New Testament. "And as it is appointed unto men once to die, but after this the judgment"

(Hebrews 9:27). The obviously subjective nature of this near death experience and the often leading nature of the questions asked of participants should raise a red flag that this phenomenon is being promoted according to a distinctly non-Christian agenda.

Examining Claims that NDE Experiences Are Always Positive

Many of the recent best-sellers on this subject have written that virtually everyone has a positive experience. For example, in his book *Life After Life* Dr. Raymond Moody wrote,

> Through all my research I have not heard a single reference to a Heaven or a Hell anything like the customary picture to which we are exposed in this society. Indeed, many persons have stressed how unlike their experiences were to what they had been led to experience in their religious training. . . . In most cases, the reward punishment model of the afterlife is abandoned and disavowed, even by many who had been accustomed to thinking in these terms.

Moody also wrote that "in the mass of material I have collected no one has ever described to me a state like the archetypical Hell."[17] Psychologist Dr. Kenneth Ring, who wrote *Life at Death: A Scientific Investigation of the Near Death Experience*, told an interviewer, "I can't recall any case of someone reporting being judged by God."[18]

The view that people only have positive experiences is contradicted also by others who have undergone a more "hellish" NDE. Recent research by Dr. H. Leon Green, documented in his excellent book, *If I Should Wake Before*

I Die, explores this contradiction. Dr. Maurice Rawlings and Dr. B. Greyson record as well that many individuals experience a distinctly judgmental, frightening, and hell-like near-death experience that makes a profound impression on them. I highly recommend Dr. Green's book for anyone who wishes to explore this evidence more deeply.[19]

Negative Near Death Experiences

Even though a number of independent researchers have recorded that some NDE patients did have distinctly hellish spiritual experiences, almost all of the popular writers on the subject choose to ignore such cases.[20]

Dr. Maurice S. Rawlings, who was a cardiologist working in the Diagnostic Center in Chattanooga, Tennessee, actually discovered a profound faith in Jesus Christ after an extremely troubling near death experience, The dying patient kept screaming as he was dying, "I am in Hell!" Doctor Rawlings wrote that his distressed patient returned to consciousness several times, but would repeatedly lose consciousness whenever his chest was not compressed. The patient's eyes would then roll upward, his back would arch, his breathing would stop, and he would once again "die." Every time his dying patient regained consciousness, heartbeat, and respiration, he would loudly scream, "I am in Hell!" In his abject terror he would plead that his doctor somehow save him from the threat of Hell. The patient begged, "Don't you understand? I am in Hell. Each time you quit I go back to Hell! Don't let me go back to Hell! . . ." Frightened by these desperate words, the doctor began rigorous efforts to save his patient's life. The patient repeatedly begged his doctor to save him from the Hell that the Scriptures affirmed was the judgment of God that awaited him only moments away, "How do I stay out of Hell?"

Although Dr. Rawlings was only a nominal Christian at this time, he finally agreed to pray with his patient that God would save him from Hell. Dr. Rawlings wrote that he reluctantly prayed aloud as he continued to treat his patient. "Lord Jesus, I ask you to keep me out of Hell. Forgive my sins. I turn my life over to you. If I die, I want to go to Heaven. If I live, I'll be on the hook forever." After three recurrences of clinical death and unconsciousness from the loss of heartbeat and respiration, the patient was taken to a hospital where he finally recovered. The doctor was distressed by the incident and returned to his home. He picked up his old Bible and began to study its ancient truths.

Later, Dr. Rawlings admitted that the incident had terrified him. Ultimately, he wrote a book revealing the fact that many dying patients underwent fearful "hell-like" near death experiences that were not being properly recorded. His book *Beyond Death's Door*, written in 1978, explored his observations of patients as they were resuscitated following their clinical death. Dr. Rawlings reported many accounts of patients who described to him very unpleasant scenes involving grotesque animals and human figures, the sounds of people groaning in pain, and visions of violence, demons, and torture. In contradiction to most other researchers, Dr. Rawlings concluded that just as many participants had a hellish experience as a positive one.[21]

The Scriptures, however, make clear that humans do not experience the judgment of Hell immediately after death. No one goes to Hell until they first appear before the Great White Throne Judgement that will occur in Heaven after the end of the future one-thousand-year Millennium that follows the Battle of Armageddon. Therefore, if these hellish NDEs actually reflect a spiritual reality, then they must be scenes in *hades*, the place of waiting for those who reject Christ's salvation. Dr. Rawling's second book, *Before Death Comes*, published in 1980, includes many additional reports of patients describing hellish NDEs. This book has annoyed many NDE authors by encouraging people to repent of their sins and accept Jesus Christ as their personal Savior if they wish "to die a good death" and avoid the horrors of Hell.

Dangerous Teachings

The Bible repeatedly warns believers that Satan will attempt to deceive us in order to destroy our souls. For example, the Gospel of Matthew teaches, "Enter ye in at the strait gate: for wide is the gate, and broad is the way, that leadeth to destruction, and many there be which go in thereat: Because strait is the gate, and narrow is the way, which leadeth unto life, and few there be that find it" (Matthew 7:13–14). Matthew also recorded Christ's final prophecy before His crucifixion in which He warned Christians specifically about the spiritual deception that would arise in the last days: "For there shall arise false Christs, and false prophets, and shall show great signs and wonders; insomuch that, if it were possible, they shall deceive the very elect" (Matthew 24:24). Obviously, the spiritual dangers He warns about are great because the deception is so effective that it causes many to fall. The Scriptures warn us that Satan himself is able to disguise himself as an angel of light to deceive any who will listen. The apostle Paul warns, "And no marvel; for Satan himself is transformed into an angel of light" (2 Corinthians 11:14).

A very critical editorial about near death experiences appeared in the well-respected magazine *Christianity Today* in 1976. The writer warned Christians about uncritically accepting the spiritual implications of the almost universally positive near death experiences reported by people who have no faith in God.

> Before Christians jump on the bandwagon or add this data to their apologetic arsenal, they should be aware that no essential difference is reported between the OBEs (out of body experiences) of believers and unbelievers! All testify to a distinctively positive experience — a feeling of perfect peace, floating outside the body, restoration to wholeness, hearing beautiful music, and the like. Christians testify to seeing Christ; Hindus say they come face to face with Krishna. Cultists tend to have their world view validated, and some nominal Christians adopt heterodox opinions.[22]

Anyone seriously interested in finding the truth should carefully consider the startling differences between the teachings of the Bible and the radically opposing claims of proponents of most NDEs. We must consider the question of whether the strange "being of light" that some patients claim to have met might actually be Satan himself, or one of his demons, disguising himself to deceive people about the urgent need to repent of their sin.

Many of the participants report seeing a "being of light," and often have assumed that it was God or Christ who told them that there is no Hell or punishment to fear.[23] Kenneth Ring reported in his study that participants, while in the presence of the light, felt that "all sins were forgiven."[24] However, it is clear that this being of light cannot possibly be Jesus Christ or God the Father; God cannot and will not contradict Himself. The book of Hebrews declares, "Jesus Christ the same yesterday, and today, and for ever"

(Hebrews 13:8). Jesus Himself warned us about the awesome danger of Hell in the New Testament, "Fear him, which after he hath killed hath power to cast into Hell; yea, I say unto you, Fear him" (Luke 12:5).

Another serious concern is the open and acknowledged connection between the New Age teachings of the occult and the universalist salvation teaching that is popularized in most of these books. Many of the NDE authors openly espouse New Age beliefs in reincarnation, out-of-body experiences, universalism, spiritualism, and other occult phenomena. For example, Dr. Karlis Osis, a major researcher of NDEs and of parapsychology, has declared that the near death experience, "tends to confirm much of the picture gained through mediumship."[25]

Betty Eadie's bestseller, *Embraced By The Light* was actually published in two versions — one for the Mormons, which stressed Mormon beliefs, and one that was toned down to target a larger secular audience. Other popular books on the NDE, such as Melvin Morse's *Closer To The Light* and Dr. Raymond Moody's *Life After Life*, promote New Age values and beliefs. Moody even suggests that people should attempt to communicate with the dead. The Bible condemns such practices: "Regard not them that have familiar spirits, neither seek after wizards, to be defiled by them: I am the Lord your God" (Leviticus 19:31). From these examples, it is obvious that discernment is necessary when examining this fascinating phenomenon. We must evaluate carefully the NDE claims in the light of the Scriptures' warnings about spiritual deception in the last days. The apostle Paul warns us that Satan, the enemy of all humans, continually attempts to deceive us about the need for salvation by falsely presenting "another Jesus," and "another gospel." Paul wrote:

> But I fear, lest by any means, as the serpent beguiled Eve through his subtlety, so your minds should be corrupted from the simplicity that is in Christ. For if he that cometh preacheth another Jesus, whom we have not preached, or if ye receive another spirit, which ye have not received, or another gospel, which ye have not accepted, ye might well bear with him" (2 Corinthians 11:3–4)

The apostle Paul's letter to the church in Galatia also warns that Satan attempts to deceive us by presenting "another Gospel," one that contradicts the genuine salvation message of Jesus Christ that is taught in the four canonical Gospels in the New Testament.

> I marvel that ye are so soon removed from him that called you into the grace of Christ unto another gospel: Which is not another; but there be some that trouble you, and would pervert the gospel of Christ. But though we, or an angel from Heaven, preach any other gospel unto you than that which we have preached unto you, let him be accursed. As we said before, so say I now again, If any man preach any other gospel unto you than that ye have received, let him be accursed. (Galatians 1:6–9)

In another epistle Paul specifically warns that "in the last days perilous times shall come" and there will be many people who will have "a form of godliness, but denying the power thereof: from such turn away" (2 Timothy 3:1, 5). Clearly, this philosophy of universal salvation is "another gospel," a gospel that totally contradicts the genuine Gospel of Jesus Christ. Who but Satan would desire to confuse and deceive millions of humans about the absolute need for personal repentance and faith in Christ's atonement for our sins? Consider the inspired warning of the apostle Paul about the "strong delusion" that would arise in the last days to assault our beliefs in the need for faith in Christ, holiness, and personal salvation:

> And then shall that Wicked be revealed, whom the Lord shall consume with the spirit of his mouth, and shall destroy with the brightness of his coming: Even him, whose coming is after the working of Satan with all power and signs and lying wonders, And with all deceivableness of unrighteousness in them that perish; because they received not the love of the truth, that they might be saved. And for this cause God shall send them strong delusion, that they should believe a lie: That they all might be damned who believed not the truth, but had pleasure in unrighteousness. (2 Thessalonians 2:8–12)

Paul warns that this spiritual deception will actually tear some away from their faith in Christ: "Now the Spirit speaketh expressly, that in the latter times some shall depart from the faith, giving heed to seducing spirits, and doctrines of devils" (1 Timothy 4:1).

Ultimately, the widespread claims about near death experiences reported by so many people around the world who have no personal agenda suggests that some people do have a genuine experience. This implies that our souls do survive the physical death of our body. However, if we want to discover additional truth about the nature of our spiritual life after death, we must find a more authoritative source — someone who truly died and then returned from the dead after a period of several days. If such a person could clearly describe the truth about the condition and future existence of the spirits of those who die, we would finally have the answer to the most important and most controversial question of all. That person is Jesus of Nazareth. In a later chapter we will examine His statements and claims about this subject.

Notes

1. John Weldon and Zola Levitt, *Is There Life After Death?* (Dallas: Zola Levitt Ministries, 1990).
2. Plato, *The Last Days of Socrates,* Trans. Hugh Tredennick (Baltimore: Penguin Books, 1959) 75.
3. Raymond A. Moody, *Life After Life* (New York: Bantam Books, 1975).
4. Raymond A. Moody, *Journal of the American Medical Association* July 1979.
5. Raymond A. Moody, *Reflections on Life After Life* (New York: Bantam Books, 1977).
6. Machael B. Sabom, *Recollections of Death: A Medical Investigation* (New York: Harper & Row, 1982).
7. *Journal of the American Medical Association* July 1979.
8. "Near Death Experiences," *Toronto Star* 5 March 2000.
9. *National Post* 4 Feb. 2000.
10. *Toronto Star* 5 March 2000.
11. Raymond A. Moody, *The Light Beyond* (New York: Bantam Books, 1988) 33–56.
12. P. M. H. Atwater, *Beyond The Light* (New York: Avon Books, 1995) 144.
13. Kenneth Ring, *Heading Toward Omega* (New York: William Morrow, 1985) 94–98.
14. *National Post* 4 Feb. 2000.
15. B. Greyson, "The Near-Death Experience Scale. Construction, Reliability, and Validity," *Journal of Nervous and Mental Disease* (1983): 369–375.
16. F. Schoonmaker, "Denver Cardiologist Discloses Findings after 18 Years of Near-Death Research," *Anabiosis* 1 (1979): 1–2.
17. Raymond A. Moody, *Reflections on Life After Life* (New York: Bantam Books, 1977).

18. J. White, "Beyond The Body: An Interview with Kenneth Ring," *Science of Mind* Nov. 1988: 89, rpt. in *Christian Research Journal* Spring 1992: 4.
19. H. Leon Green, *If I Should Wake Before I Die* (Wheaton: Crossway Books, 1997).
20. P. M. H. Atwater, *Beyond The Light* (New York: Avon Books, 1994) 30–45.
21. Maurice Rawlings, *Beyond Death's Door* (New York: Thomas Nelson, Inc., 1978) 18–20.
22. "Scientific Evidence for Life After Death?" *Christianity Today* 27 Aug. 1976: 21.
23. Raymond A. Moody, *Reflections on Life After Life* (New York: Bantam Books, 1977).
24. Kenneth Ring, *Heading Toward Omega* (New York: William Morrow, 1985) 224.
25. John White, "What The Dying See," *Psychic* Sept./Oct. 1976: 40.

5

Deathbed Visions

Throughout history many dying people have experienced deathbed visions. Many of these final visions have been recorded by doctors, nurses, and family, especially during the last few centuries. These visions often include a scene in which the individual reports seeing a friend or family member who has been absent from their life for a period of time. Often it turns out that this loved one has actually died previously, unbeknownst to the dying person. In addition to describing a vision of some departed loved one, or a vision of the next life, many dying patients express a strong feeling of spiritual and emotional elation, feelings proved to be unrelated to the drugs administered to them. Most of these deathbed visions last between three and five minutes. As many as 50 percent of those who have had such visions also experience a glimpse of their spiritual life after death. Interestingly, the likelihood of a person experiencing such a vision does not seem to depend upon their previously held religious views about whether or not there is an afterlife. Many of those who were dying, along with their loved ones who were present at their deathbed, felt real comfort and experienced spiritual healing through the deathbed vision. These deathbed visions suggest that our life does not end at the grave. The New Testament refers to spiritual visions and "spiritual blessings in heavenly places in Christ." The apostle Paul wrote, "Blessed be the God and Father of our Lord Jesus Christ, who hath blessed us with all spiritual blessings in heavenly places in Christ" (Ephesians 1:3).

Deathbed visions were much more common in previous centuries. Until recently, most people died at home, without being administered massive amounts of pain killers and other sedatives that could make meaningful communication virtually impossible. During Dr. Melvin Morse's research, he discovered that the experience of these deathbed visions usually removed the fear of death from both the dying patient as well as their loved ones. This profound experience often helped the patient, because it allowed them to share something spiritually important with their family. Interestingly, even the medical personnel who listened to these uplifting visions received enormous spiritual benefits that helped prevent the emotional burnout that many doctors and nurses experience from witnessing patients suffer and die.[1]

Doctors and nurses verify that the modern medical practice of heavily sedating those who are dying prevents most patients from remembering or communicating clearly to others. Some doctors suggest that only about 10 percent of modern deaths occur while the patient is still fully conscious and not medicated. However, an astonishingly high percentage (over 50 percent) of those who are fully conscious when they face death actually describe deathbed visions. Equally interesting is the observation that dying people seldom weep. While the loved ones naturally grieve in anticipation of the approaching crisis, a strange calm is often felt by the one who feels the approach of death.

Voltaire, a great French philosopher and professed atheist, expressed his contempt for the fear of death and the prospect of an afterlife throughout his celebrated life. He once wrote to a woman who had expressed her own fear of approaching death, saying, "All things considered, I am of the opinion that one ought never to think of death. This thought is of no use whatsoever, save to embitter life. Death is a mere nothing. Those people who solemnly proclaim it are enemies of the human race; one must endeavor always to keep them off." However, Voltaire, the great enemy of Christianity who ridiculed those who placed their faith in Jesus Christ, finally came to the moment of his own death. As he lay on his deathbed Voltaire cried out continually that he was abandoned by God and man. He repeatedly called out in utter despair: "O Christ! Oh, Jesus Christ!" His doctor declared that it was his lot that Voltaire should die under his hands. As soon as he saw that all means he had employed to increase Voltaire's strength had just the opposite effect, death was constantly before his eyes. From that moment, madness took possession of Voltaire's soul. He expired under the torments of the furies. Voltaire's physician was so terrified that he abandoned his patient and refused to return to his patient's room. Voltaire's closest friend, the Marshal de Richelieu, another cynical atheist, was so appalled and filled with fear at witnessing his friend's mortal anguish that he also fled his friend's presence. Voltaire's nurse, who was hired to care for him in his last days, refused to ever again care for the dying because she was afraid of witnessing another scene such as the death of Voltaire.

John Wesley, the great evangelist, described in a letter to his brother Charles Wesley a visit to the deathbed of a young Christian woman. He claimed that he distinctly heard the music of angels. Wesley wrote, "I firmly believed that young woman would die in peace; though I did not apprehend it would be so soon. We have had several instances of music heard before or at the death of those that die in the Lord. May we conceive that this is, literally, the music of angels? Can that be heard by ears of flesh and blood?"[2] When Charles wrote back to him about the matter, John Wesley replied by adding the following detail: "I cannot apprehend that such music has any analogy at all to the inward voice of God. I take it to differ from this total genre, and to be rather the effect of an angel affecting the auditory nerves, as an apparition does the optic nerve, or retina."[3]

Another famous example of a compelling foretaste of Heaven is the experience reported by the Christian pastor and writer Richard Baxter in his book *Everlasting Rest of the Saints*:

> Rest! How sweet the sound! It is melody to my ears. It lies as a reviving cordial at my heart, and from thence sends forth lively spirits, which beat through all the pulses of my soul. O blessed day, when I shall rest with God, when I shall rest in the bosom of my Lord, when I shall rest in knowing, loving, rejoicing, and praising Him. O joyful sentence, 'Come, ye blessed.' O blessed grace! O blessed love! How love and joy will rise! But I cannot express it; I cannot conceive it.[4]

Pastor W. B. Clark often ministered at the bedside

of dying Christians. He wrote about his experience as follows:

> I have often thought . . . from what I have myself witnessed at a dying bed that sometimes, before the soul of the believer is disengaged from the body, the glories of Paradise are partially disclosed to his view, and the distant tones of its hymns of sweetest melody burst upon his ravished ear; that, hovering as it were midway between earth and Heaven, he catches a glimpse of the spiritual world before he leaves the material. . . . Faint not, suffering believer, the promised land is full in view before thee. . . . Be assured, this is no transient view, which is but set before thee, and then snatched away forever. Thou wilt soon be permitted to descend into the goodly land beyond Jordan, and enter the New Jerusalem with songs, and everlasting joy upon thy head.[5]

At the moment when death finally approaches, the true follower of Christ can look up from this temporary earthly vista toward our eternal heavenly home. Like the apostle John, we can also say, "I looked, and behold a door was opened in Heaven!" (Revelation 4:1) At that final moment when the veil is cast aside we will begin to see with our spiritual eyes our first glimpse of the heavenly New Jerusalem. Then we shall finally appreciate the full meaning of the Gospel's record of Christ's transfiguration: "As He prayed, the fashion of his countenance was altered" (Luke 9:29). Matthew tells us that Christ was "transfigured before them: and his face did shine as the sun, and his raiment was white as the light" (Matthew 17:2).

For the Christian, death represents a triumph over our present trials and tribulations, our pain and discomfort.

Finally, all of our earthly conflicts and sufferings are left behind as we enter into that blessed rest that our Lord has prepared for us. The psalmist David caught a glimpse of that glorious moment when we shall enter into Christ's final victory and His eternal glory: "Lift up your heads, O ye gates; even lift them up, ye everlasting doors; and the King of glory shall come in" (Psalms 24:9).

A nineteenth-century doctor named David Nelson became a firm believer in Jesus Christ after listening to the final comments of many of his patients on their deathbed. Dr. Nelson wrote about the impact of these experiences:

> First, I have known those, the cases are not unfrequent, who were brave, who had stood unflinching in battle's whirlpool. They had resolved never to disgrace their system of unbelief by a trembling death. They had called to Christians in the tone of resolve, saying, I can die as coolly as you can. I had seen those die from whom entire firmness might fairly be expected. I had heard groans, even if the teeth were clenched for fear of complaint, such as I never wish to hear again; and I had looked into countenances, such as I hope never to see again.
>
> Again, I had seen cowards die. I had seen those depart who were naturally timid, who expected themselves to meet death with fright and alarm. I had heard such, as it were, sing before Jordan was half forded. I had seen faces where, palled as they were, I beheld more celestial triumph than I had ever witnessed anywhere else. In that voice there was a sweetness, and in that eye there was a glory, which

> I never could have fancied in the death-spasms, if I had not been near.[6]

Dr. Nelson also reported that when several of his patients were on the point of death they called out, "Catch me, I am sinking; hold me, I am falling." He wrote that others called out, "Do you hear that music? Oh, were ever notes so celestial!"[7]

Notes

1. Melvin Morse, *Closer to the Light — Learning From the Near-Death Experiences of Children* (New York: Ivy Books, 1993) 63–65.
2. John Wesley, letter, *Posthumous Pieces — John Wesley de La Fletchere* (Dublin: Robert Napier, 1802).
3. John Wesley, letter, *Posthumous Pieces — John Wesley de La Fletchere* (Dublin: Robert Napier, 1802).
4. Richard Baxter, *Everlasting Rest of the Saints* (New York: American Tract Society, 1850).
5. J. H. Potts, *Golden Dawn* (Philadelphia: P. W. Ziegler & Co., 1880).
6. David Nelson, *The Cause and Cure of Infidelity* (New York: American Tract Society, 1841) 307.
7. David Nelson, *The Cause and Cure of Infidelity* (New York: American Tract Society, 1841) 312.

6

Scientific Evidence of Immortality

The Nature of Reality

To the naked eye, our physical universe appears to be composed of extremely solid material. However, at the subatomic level, nothing could be further from the truth. All of the matter in our vast universe is composed of atoms. The protons, neutrons, and electrons of each atom spin around the nucleus at the almost inconceivable speed of light — 187,000 miles a second. However, the relative distance between the tiny nucleus at the center of the atom and the even smaller electrons in their orbit is staggering. Particle physics reveals that the distance from the nucleus to the electron circling it is equivalent to the vast distance between our sun and our earth of approximately 93 million miles. In other words, the atoms that make up everything apparently "solid" in our universe are in fact composed of 99.999999999% empty space.

Everything that exists in our known universe is composed of either energy or matter. Gigantic particle accelerators that smash nuclei into atoms at the speed of light helped scientists discover that even the incredibly small nucleus, protons, anti-protons, and electrons are, in fact, composed of energy rather than anything solid or material. The "Conservation of Energy" states that since the beginning of the universe nothing is able to be created or destroyed — it can only be transformed from one form into another. This scientific theory has no known exceptions. Nuclear fission for example transforms radioactive uranium 235 into extraordinary amounts of heat, sound, and explosive energy. Since everything that exists in our universe must be either matter or energy, it seems certain that our mind and our spirit must be composed of some kind of energy. Logically, if our soul is some form of energy, then it too cannot be destroyed; it can only be transformed into some other form of energy. In 1929 the writer Reverand John Haynes Holmes expressed this thought in his book, *Ten Reasons for Believing in Immortality*: "nothing in the universe is ever lost. All energy is conserved . . . the energy persists if not in the old form then in a new one," and the sum total of energy remains unchanged.

When we take into consideration that our universe, our earth, and our bodies are composed primarily of empty space and tiny particles of energy spinning at the speed of light, it is easier to understand how the nonmaterial human spirit could survive the physical dissolution of the human body. Edinburgh University astrophysicist Professor Michael Scott wrote, "The advancement of quantum physics has produced a description of reality which allows the existence of parallel universes. Composed of real substances they could not interact with matter from our own universe." In his book *Mind and the New Physics*, Professor Fred Alan Wolf states, "As fantastic as it sounds, the new physics called quantum mechanics posits that there exists, side by side with this world, another world, a parallel universe, a duplicate copy that is somehow slightly different yet the same."[1]

The Evidence of God and Immortality

Anyone who seriously considers the question of immortality and the possibility of an afterlife for the human spirit quickly realizes that these issues are tied directly to the question of the existence of God. If a supernatural God exists then it is logical to consider the possibility that He created our human spirits to live forever. However, if God does not exist then it is extremely likely that our souls are not immortal and that life does end at the grave. It is remarkable that after a century and a half of scientific denial of the existence of God a multitude of scientists are now acknowledging that our universe contains astonishing evidence that only a supernatural Designer could possibly have designed our galaxy, solar system, and planet to allow life to flourish on earth.

For many centuries the obvious examples of design present in our world including the rotation of the planets and the intricate complexity in organs such as the eye or ear provided ample evidence to convince many that there must be an intelligent Designer. Sir Isaac Newton, the great scientist, wrote, "the most beautiful system of the sun, planets and comets could only proceed from the counsel and dominion of an intelligent and powerful Being."[2] He also wrote that "the mere Laws of Nature" could never themselves be the cause for the order we see in the world to "arise out of a Chaos."[3]

The Argument From Design

An English philosopher, Reverend William Paley (1743–1805), wrote an important book entitled *Natural Theology* (1817) in which he developed a powerful "argument from design" that proves the necessity of an all-powerful designer to account for the awesome complexity apparent in all of nature. "Contrivance must have had a contriver — design, a designer." Paley used the example of a man finding a watch with a beautiful design and exquisite craftmanship lying in a field. He argued that the existence of the watch provided persuasive evidence of intelligent design that could never have occurred as a result of random chance. No rational man finding such a watch in a field would ever conclude that the materials arranged themselves together into a watch that could keep perfect time by random chance over many years. Even an eye aided by a common microscope can see that the biological complexity of the organisms of living creatures far exceeds the design of the most wonderful watch ever built by a Swiss watchmaker. As Paley wrote, ". . . the contrivances of nature surpass the contrivances of art, in the complexity, subtlety, and curiosity of the mechanism."

However, the development of the theory of evolution by Sir Charles Darwin that was furthered by his monumental book *The Origin of Species* in 1859 seemed to provide atheists with another possible answer to account for the overwhelming complexity and obvious order that is present in all biological life forms. Darwin's theory of natural selection, the "survival of the fittest," suggested that over long periods of time random mutations and variations would appear by pure chance. Those mutations that provided a biological advantage to a living creature would tend to improve the survivability of that organism. Since such an entity would have an advantage it would tend to live longer and breed more successfully. Thus it would transmit its genes, including the new mutation, to its offspring. The theory is that such minute genetic mutations would, over vast amounts of time, gradually improve and transform a species to the point that entirely new organs and biological features would develop into a new, more complex species. According to Darwin and the many evolutionary scientists who followed him, natural selection alone can account for the gradual improvement of a particular species and the development of increasingly complex and new species over vast lengths of time without any need of an intelligent Designer. If evolution is to be a workable theory then it must be demonstrated by the scientists that random chance mutations can somehow add additional useful information to the genetic code passed from parent to offspring to account for the theoretical evolution toward greater complexity. However, one of the greatest problems with this theory of evolution is that *not one positive mutation has ever been observed* and recorded in the last century and a half of biological observations. The failure to demonstrate any pattern of positive mutations stands as enormously powerful evidence against the possibility of evolution.

While the evolutionary theory gained almost universal scientific acceptance over the last century and a half, the incredible discoveries of modern biology, especially the discovery of the awesome complexity of the DNA genetic code that is the blueprint for all biological organisms and life forms, has demonstrated that Darwinian evolutionary theory is impossible. Modern scientists discovered that the amount of information transmitted by the DNA genetic code is so complex that it is simply impossible that this information could have accumulated by random chance without an intelligent Creator. The DNA genetic code is arranged as a double helix coiled within every one of our trillions of individual cells. In fact every one of our cells contains the encoded information to recreate our complete body and repair its organs if they are damaged. Every single cell in our body contains over six billion nucleotides that contain the complete blueprint to recreate and repair our body. The DNA gene sequence contains so much complex information that if the information in a single cell was expressed in an alphabetical form it would fill over two thousand volumes with each of them containing a thousand pages of data. If the DNA double helix in each cell was uncoiled it would stretch more than four inches in length.

For example, Dr. A. E. Wilder-Smith wrote about the awesome complexity of the biological cells:

> It is astonishing that God creates human beings with the entire genetic coded information to produce a new human implanted into two microscopic reproductive cells, the sperm and egg cells. The double helix DNA sequence that contains the encoding to determine every one of your trillions of cells, every organ, and function is replicated in every one of your fifty billion cells. In addition, the DNA contains the complete genetic information to construct your body as well as repair it if it is injured. If one were to request an engineer to accomplish this feat of information miniaturization, one would be considered fit for the psychiatric clinic.[4]

The discovery of incredibly complex genetic information

patterns encoded within the double helix DNA genetic code that governs all biological life forms provides overwhelming evidence that an intelligent designer must have created this DNA. Professor Geisler wrote about the significance of the DNA information patterns, "It is scientifically necessary to point to intelligence as the cause of the first living cell." A great deal of additional information that proves the impossibility of the theory of evolution is documented in my earlier book *The Handwriting of God*.

A more powerful argument against the atheistic concept of an accidental universe and the development of human life has been discovered in the last several decades. This information has been widely publicized and debated within scientific circles. Numerous articles have appeared in scientific publications as well as Internet discussion groups for scientists. However, this revolutionary information has not yet been widely publicized within the general media nor has the information been given to high school teachers who teach our children that "there is no evidence for the existence of God."

The Anthropic Principle

The scientific discovery in the last few decades of the astonishing degree of precision in the principles and elements of our universe design by modern scientists now provides an overwhelming argument that the universe was "fine tuned" to an extraordinary degree. The only logical explanation for this precise "fine tuning" is the acceptance that a supernaturally intelligent being must have precisely designed the universe to allow stars, planets, hydrogen, carbon, and the necessary conditions for human life to exist. The discovery that the physical characteristics of the known universe provide overwhelming evidence that our universe was designed in a very precise manner to allow human life to flourish is now known as the Anthropic Principle. In short, this theory suggests that the recent discoveries of modern science have found there are an extraordinary number of elements of design that are evident in our universe and solar system that could not possibly have occurred by random chance. In fact, the evidence provides compelling proof that our universe and the earth itself were designed by a supernaturally intelligent being with the purpose of developing human life upon the planet earth.

During the last fifty years a multitude of scientists have discovered that it is virtually impossible that the universe, the solar system, the earth, and humans developed by random chance. The overwhelming evidence from science proves that an astonishing number of aspects of our universe were precisely fine tuned in such a way that would allow human life to flourish on this planet. The Anthropic Principle simply acknowledges that the universe appears to be precisely designed by some great intelligence to provide for the well-being of humanity. This discovery of extraordinary evidence of supernatural design is producing a genuine intellectual revolution in the world of science. The Anthropic Principle has been documented in numerous scientific books and articles but is still not well known by educators or the general public. However, as the general population learns about this remarkable discovery it has the capacity to transform the thinking of our society in many areas including the understanding that we are not the result of an accident in a universe without meaning and purpose. As the evidence will demonstrate, our universe, our world, and life itself could never have existed unless a supreme intelligence had designed every aspect of the universe to allow human life to exist.

Scientists were initially astonished when they began to discover the numerous ways in which every scientific law, principle, and fundamental constant was "fine tuned" to such a degree that allowed the universe to function as it does. Even the slightest variation of these laws and principles would result in a universe that would not contain stars, planets, or life itself. The evidence is overwhelming that if any of these scientific constants were changed by the smallest degree then life would not exist.

For example, astronomers have precisely measured the speed with which the galaxies are rapidly moving apart. This expansion rate of the universe is precisely the correct speed to allow our galaxy and planet to exist. If the expansion rate were any faster no galaxies would ever have formed. On the other hand, if the expansion rate were any slower the force of gravity would have caused the universe to collapse before any stars or galaxies could form. Professor Robert Dicke reported that a decrease in the speed of expansion by even one part in a million as the universe initially exploded would have caused it to collapse within seconds of creation.[5] The average distance between the stars in our galaxy is precisely what is required for our planet to exist. If the stars were farther apart, the necessary amount of heavy elements essential to form a rocky planet would not reach our earth. If the stars were closer it would massively disrupt the planetary orbit, making life impossible.

Two of the most fundamental scientific constants that determine the nature of our universe and life itself are the force of gravity and the strong nuclear force. This strong nuclear force holds together the sub-atomic particles in the nucleus of all atoms. If this force were even a fraction weaker then all other atoms except for hydrogen could not exist, which would make our universe and life impossible.

However, if the strong nuclear force were even slightly stronger hydrogen atoms would have formed only rarely and all of the heavy elements essential to life would not exist either.

Another example of purposeful design is apparent in the nature of supernova eruptions of dying stars that occur occasionally throughout the galaxy and shower our planet with heavy elements that are essential for the formation of a rocky planet like earth as well as for the formation of the chemistry of life. If such supernova explosions occurred more frequently or too close to our planet all life would be exterminated by excessive radiation. If there were far fewer supernova eruptions or they were much farther away the planet would not have the necessary heavy elements required for life to exist. Even the mass of our sun is precisely calibrated to allow life to flourish. If the sun possessed greater mass then it would have burned far too rapidly. But if the sun possessed less mass the ultra-violet radiation would be insufficient to allow plant life to produce sugar and oxygen. The distance between the sun and earth is also of the precise amount to sustain plant and animal life. If the sun was only one percent farther from the surface of the earth it would be too cool to sustain vegetation as well as balanced level of precipitation, which is essential for life. However, if the sun was even five percent closer to the earth the level of precipitation would be unstable and the earth's surface would be too hot to allow vegetation and human life to prosper.

Gravity is one of the fundamental forces that governs our universe including the earth's orbit about the sun as well as the moon's orbit around our planet. When Isaac Newton first determined the critical importance of gravity three centuries ago his formula for the strength of gravity demonstrated that all matter was attracted to other matter with a degree of force that was inversely proportional to the square of the distance separating the objects. Newton calculated that one of the factors in the mathematical formula for gravitation is precisely the number 2. Scientists have often wondered why this factor should be precisely 2 and not some approximation of that number. However, the latest research with sophisticated devices confirms that the factor is precisely 2 and does not deviate from this to an astonishing degree of precision. In fact, it does not differ from 2 by even one part in 10,000.[6]

Any variation from the precise value of 2 would result in a disastrous degradation of the orbits of the earth, moon, and other planets and would make life impossible. The surface gravity of our planet is exquisitely balanced to the exact amount that allows life to exist. If the surface gravity was greater the ammonia and methane gases would not escape the atmosphere and make life impossible. On the other hand, if gravity was weaker then the essential water vapor in our atmosphere would escape and life would cease.

Another curious factor is that water is the only known substance that expands when it freezes, causing it to float on the surface rather than sinking to the bottom. If water did not possess this unusual quality ice would slowly sink to the bottom of a lake or ocean killing all biological entities including fish. Other examples of purposeful design include the Gulf Stream, which forms an enormous warm underwater river that warms the climate of Europe and prevents it from becoming frozen like Greenland. Incredibly, the waters of the Gulf Stream do not dispearse in the North Atlantic as you would expect. The edge of this massive deep ocean river is so precise that the temperature will be significantly warmer in the Gulf Stream compared to the surrounding ocean waters only twenty feet away.

Another remarkable example of intelligent design is found in the lightning that often frightens us. Without lightning, life on earth would be impossible. Scientists discovered that every lightning bolt instantaneously superheats the surrounding air to extremely high temperatures. As the air begins to immediately cool, the extreme heat causes nitrogen and oxygen molecules in the air to combine as nitrogen dioxide, which immediately dissolves in the rain to form nitric acid. This is converted into nitrates that fertilize the ground when it falls to the earth allowing vegetation to flourish and animal life to exist. Every lightning bolt produces over one hundred pounds of nitrogen dioxide. According to climatologists, over a hundred lightning bolts hit the planet every single second producing over fifty percent of nitrogen oxide that is absolutely essential for vegetation and human life.

Even the axial tilt of the planet at 23 degrees has been proven to be essential to allow life to prosper. If this tilt of the planet was significantly greater the surface temperature of the planet would prevent life from continuing. But if the tilt were less, vegetation would suffer greatly because the difference in surface temperatures would be far too great. The rotation speed of the planet every twenty-four hours also appears to be calculated with intelligent purpose. If the earth rotated more slowly the earth's surface would experience huge temperature differences between long periods of darkness and light that would make it impossible for vegetation to flourish. Likewise, if the earth rotated much more quickly than it does, the speed of the atmospheric winds would be incredibly destructive.

Climatic scientists have discovered that our atmosphere

contains precisely the right mixture of gases to allow life to exist. If there were more carbon dioxide than exists now there would be an extremely rapid acceleration of plant growth that would disrupt normal life. However, if the level of carbon dioxide in the atmosphere was significantly less than it is, vegetation would die because plants could not utilize photosynthesis to function normally.

In total, more than fifty different scientific principles and laws have been discovered that were designed and fine tuned to absolutely precise limits to permit our universe, galaxy, solar system, planet, and human life to exist and flourish. These discoveries provide compelling evidence that our universe was created by a supernaturally intelligent Creator.

In light of these remarkable scientific discoveries regarding the nature of matter and energy in our universe, the probability of the energy of our nonmaterial spirit surviving the death of our physical body becomes more and more plausible. Dr. Werner von Braun, the great German missile scientist who created the American space program after WWII, wrote about his personal conclusions on immortality. Thomas Pynchon quotes Dr. von Braun in the opening pages of his novel *Gravity's Rainbow*: "Nature does not know extinction: all it knows is transformation. Everything science has taught me and continues to teach me, strengthens my belief in the continuity of spiritual experience after death."

Life After Death

Death is that point in time when the spirit separates "permanently" from the body. However, we cannot always be certain about the exact moment death occurs. Does it happen the second the body ceases to breathe? Decades ago, doctors confidently referred to the principle "Where there is no breath, there is no life." However, in the last few decades, because of the remarkable medical advances in emergency trauma care, many patients who have ceased breathing for a few minutes, or occasionally for several hours, have been revived to full health. This is possible especially when the body has been subjected to a significant drop in temperature due to exposure or drowning in cold water. The development of sophisticated medical resuscitation techniques and powerful drugs have allowed paramedics and emergency room doctors to revive many patients from death, whereas years ago they would have slipped away forever.

The Atheist's Objection: The Soul Cannot Exist Without the Body

One of the greatest objections to the survival of the soul is the belief that the mind-soul depends upon the brain and body for its continuing function and existence. This idea is summarized articulately by Colin McGinn:

> What we call 'the mind' is in fact made up a great number of sup-capacities, and each of these depends upon the functioning of the brain. Now, the facts of neurology compellingly demonstrate . . . that everything about the mind, from the sensory-motor periphery to the inner sense of self, is minutely controlled by the brain: if your brain lacks certain chemicals or gets locally damaged, your mind is apt to fall apart at the seams. . . . If parts of the mind depend for their existence upon parts of the brain, then the whole of the mind

> must so depend too. Hence the soul dies with the brain, which is to say it is mortal.[7]

This idea that "the soul dies with the brain, which is to say it is mortal" seems at first glance to be plausible. Obviously the mind is strongly affected by brain function; it can change through disease, drugs, and tumors. However, the soul is not identical with the mind. For example, while the mind of a baby is very limited in its perceptions and mental functions, its soul is fully formed from the time that life begins. Likewise, although the mind of an older person can be tragically impaired by devastating diseases such as Alzheimer's, the soul of the person remains whole despite its inability to express itself.

Furthermore, even the concept that the mind cannot exist without the active functioning of the brain is now being challenged by new laboratory research and unusual medical cases. A number of remarkable experiments and medical emergencies have provided compelling new evidence that the boundary between life and death is not nearly as well defined as we formerly thought. There have been numerous cases of almost miraculous restorations to life of individuals who were drowned in cold water for extended periods. In addition, a number of exceptional cases have occurred recently that raise profound questions about the dividing line between life and death. These cases suggest that the mind-soul can both exist and retain memories as well as knowledge, even when the brain is not functioning. These discoveries strongly support the concept that the soul has an independent existence from the body and that it could survive death.

Medical Experiments That Suggest Immortality

Dr. Paul Segal of the University of California at Berkley altered the brain-cell chemistry of rats by drastically reducing the protein in their diet. Incredibly, this diet change dramatically slowed the aging process within the cells and doubled the normal life span of these rats. This experiment tended to confirm the results of an earlier experiment in 1932 that revealed a doubling of the life span of rats when their diet was altered to reduce the number of calories they consumed each day. Dr. Segal speculates that potentially we could live for hundreds of years if our cells could maintain the level of vigor that is normal during our teen years and build a strong auto-immune system to fight against disease.

In another fascinating experiment, Dr. Segal painlessly killed a hamster at the University of California's science lab by lowering its body temperature. He then kept its body frozen for hours by packing it in ice. During four hours of continuous freezing, sensitive electrical monitors determined that there was no brain or heart activity in the hamster. Dr. Segal then heated the frozen body with a simple lamp, and the hamster began to move its legs and breathe with the initial help of a tube pumping air into its lungs. When the hamster's body returned to normal temperature, all of its body functions returned to normal. Incredibly, this experiment was successfully repeated five times over several years on the same poor hamster. The fact that a laboratory animal can return to life with its memory and life intact, after hours of clinical death, provides persuasive evidence that life can exist for a time independent of a physical body.[8]

Retention of Memory after Resuscitation

Dr. Audrey U. Smith, from the National Institute for Medical Research, Mill Hill, London, U.K., also conducted research with golden hamsters that were revived after being frozen for hours. Despite the frozen rigidity of their bodies and the fact that over 50 percent of the water in the brain of each hamster had changed to ice, these hamsters were also revived under a heat lamp, apparently to resume a normal life.[9] These experiments prove that mental functions can apparently survive both freezing and thawing. Dr. Smith also reported the retention of memory after the cessation of brain function in the frozen animals:

> We found, in collaboration with animal psychologists, that rats which had been trained to solve problems of finding food in mazes showed no appreciable loss of memory after cooling to a body temperature just above freezing. . . Activity of the cerebral cortex, as judged by electroencephalograms, ceases at about +18°C in the rat, so that cerebral activity must have been arrested for a 1–2 hour period in all the animals tested. After re-animation they were, nevertheless, capable of acting on previous experience. This result was not consistent with the theory that memory depends upon a continuous passage of nerve impulses through actively metabolizing neurons in the brain.[10]

This retention of memory after the brain has been frozen strongly suggests that the mind can exist and retain memory apart from a functioning physical brain.

Dr. Smith's experiments involved cold baths and cold packs, while the hamsters were resuscitated with simple artificial respiration and microwave heating. Professors Andjus and J. E. Lovelock have reported that their experiments with rats demonstrated the recovery and long-term survival of well over 80 percent of the animals exposed to ice cold conditions.[11] Outdoor experiments with clams in northern seas demonstrated that they also survived, despite the fact they were repeatedly frozen solid and then thawed twice each day.[12] In addition, Professor J. R. Kenyon subjected laboratory dogs to freezing temperatures until their heartbeats and circulation ceased completely. Remarkably, the dogs sufficiently recovered to the point that they survived for weeks after the initial experiment.[13]

Other researchers have frozen embryo chicken hearts, after treatment with a glycerol solution, to –19°C. Later, they applied heat to thaw these hearts. Dr. D. K. C. MacDonald from the University of Ottawa, an expert in low-temperature physics, wrote, "Perhaps the day will come when, if you want it, you can arrange to 'hibernate' for a thousand years or so in liquid air, and then be 'wakened up' again to see how the world has changed in the meantime."[14]

These experiments are extremely thought-provoking. Scientists previously believed that our consciousness, memory, and personal identity was entirely dependent upon the continuing electrical chemical interactions among the trillions of neural synapses in our brains. These experiments demonstrated that laboratory animals and humans can both resume a normal life, despite the fact that their brains were unable to function in any detectable way for a period of several hours when subjected to very low body temperatures. These experiments profoundly challenge the prevailing materialistic view of human consciousness that governs modern medicine and science. At the least, these extraordinary scientific and medical discoveries challenge us to seriously consider the possibility that our soul or spirit can survive and continue to exist after death.

Revival After Death

An article in the *Globe and Mail* newspaper (January 28, 2000) reported the remarkable case of an unnamed 29-year-old Norwegian skier who fell while she was skiing through a deep gully in Norway. She ended up wedged between the rocks and a ridge of overhanging ice. This ice continually poured freezing water over her face for at least forty minutes until she drowned. When her skiing companions finally discovered her dead and partially frozen body, they used their cell phone to call for paramedics. Unfortunately, the remote rugged location delayed medical efforts for another hour until the paramedics could arrive by helicopter and air-lift her body to a hospital.

One of her doctors, Dr. Mads Gilbert, at Tromso University Hospital confirmed that the ice-cold water had cooled her body until her heart stopped beating. The woman had clinically died, with no discernible brain function or respiration. Dr. Gilbert stated, "She was clinically dead for a couple of hours." Fortunately, the cold water cooled her brain enough so that it could exist for several hours without oxygen without undergoing cellular deterioration. When the paramedics brought her body to the hospital, all life signs had ceased. Despite the indications that she was dead, the doctors performed heroic medical measures, including a cardiopulmonary bypass. They removed the blood from her body, heated it, and then intravenously returned the warmed blood back to her body. Amazingly, after several hours of being clinically dead, her heart finally responded and began to beat again. She was initially paralyzed by the ordeal and spent sixty days in an intensive-care unit of the hospital. Thirty-five of the sixty days were spent on an artificial ventilator to assist her breathing. However, the patient managed a complete recovery and has resumed a normal life, including work . . . and even skiing.[15] If someone can die and be restored to normal life and consciousness after hours with no brain or heart function, who can say that resurrection is impossible?

In another case a five-year-old Norwegian boy named Roger Arnsten drowned during the winter of 1962. He was clinically dead for two and one half hours. For twenty-two minutes his body was floating face down in very cold water. His brain was clinically dead and his body temperature continued to fall to below 75°F, which probably prevented cellular deterioration in his brain. Dr. Tone Dahi Kvittingen tried artificial CPR, and then warm blood transfusions, despite the fact that hours had passed without heart or brain function. Incredibly, after almost two and one half hours the boy's heartbeat resumed. The boy was unconscious for over a month and a half, and then suffered temporary blindness and dementia. Fortunately, he eventually recovered almost completely.[16]

A Fascinating Scientific Experiment About Death

An intriguing scientific experiment was conducted in the early part of the 1900s by Dr. Duncan MacDougal of Haverhill, Massachusetts. This experiment was reported in *American Medicine* (April 1907). (The article is reproduced on the Internet website http://www.artbell.com/duncan.html.) Dr. MacDougal proposed an experiment to test his hypothesis that the spirit of a human, if it exists, must occupy some amount of space and, possibly, measurement. He noted that everything in our universe that occupies space, whether solid, liquid, gas, or plasma, are all subject to gravity, and therefore can be weighed. The doctor reasoned that if the spirit remains conscious and continues as a separate entity after death, then it must be composed of some substance.

His experiment consisted of placing a dying patient and his hospital bed on a platform that was a very precise scale. The apparatus was so sensitive that the loss of even one-fifth of an ounce could be detected by the platform scale beam, hitting the measuring bar audibly. Most of the patients he chose were dying of tuberculosis, which meant that they were exhausted and not moving except to breathe during their final hours. During the three hours and forty minutes until death occurred, the first patient lost one ounce per hour, as a natural result of evaporation of perspiration and moisture in his respiration. At the exact moment of death, Dr. MacDougal reported that the scale beam dropped and made "an audible stroke hitting against the lower limiting bar and remaining there with no rebound. The loss was ascertained to be three-fourths of an ounce. This loss of weight could not be due to evaporation of respiratory moisture and sweat, because that had already been determined to go on, in his case, at the rate of one-sixtieth of an ounce per minute. This new this loss was sudden and large, three-fourths of an ounce in a few seconds."[17] A number of other dying patients participated in the series of experiments, and in each completed test Dr. MacDougal reported there was a rapid and measurable loss of weight, usually between three-eighths of an ounce to one and one-half ounces, within a few seconds of the moment of death.

The article reported that the doctor carefully eliminated the possibility that loss of body fluids, etcetera, could have accounted for the weight loss, since the scale weighed the complete bed, the mattress, sheets, and patient. During the half hour following death, the doctor measured a further very gradual and continuous loss of weight as the bodily fluids evaporated from the sheets. The weight of the air expelled from the lungs at death was so small as to be negligible.

In a follow-up to his experiment on humans, Dr. MacDougal performed the same experiment on fifteen dying dogs who were observed under the same conditions of room temperature, etcetera. Intriguingly, there was no measurable loss of weight at the moment of death for any of the dogs. It is difficult to evaluate this curious experiment after so many years but it is interesting to note that there is a report about an experiment conducted in 1996 that also claimed to have measured a definite weight loss at the very moment of death. It will be interesting to see if other researchers can repeat this strange experiment.

Although the evidence we have examined thus far suggests the human spirit can survive death, it cannot reveal anything specific about the nature of our spiritual life after death, its conditions, location, and characteristics. If we are to proceed further with our examination of immortality, then we need to study someone who has died for a significant period of time, and who then was resurrected to live again. Such a person could provide unique, authoritative information about the nature of life after death and the possibility of bodily resurrection.

Fortunately, there is one person in history who makes this exceptional claim. Jesus of Nazareth is reported to have truly died and later rose from the dead. The Gospels and the Epistles of the New Testament provide historical evidence that Jesus of Nazareth rose from the dead and revealed Himself to His disciples on multiple occasions, including one appearance to over five hundred people.

These eyewitnesses were still alive thirty years after the event to confirm its historical reality. In the next chapter we will examine the evidence for this extraordinary claim and in the remaining chapters we will explore Jesus' personal statements about the nature and reality of life after death.

Notes

1. Fred Alan Wolf, *Mind and the New Physics*.
2. Isaac Newton, "Query 31," *Optics* (Chicago: University of Chicago, 1980).
3. Isaac Newton, "Query 28," *Optics* (Chicago: University of Chicago, 1980).
4. A. E. Wilder-Smith, *The Illustrated Origins Answer Book* (Gilbert: Eden Communications, 1995) 25.
5. R. H. Dicke and P. J. E. Peebles, *Hawking and Israel* (1979) 514.
6. "Gravity Very Precisely," *Science News* 5 July 1980: 13.
7. Colin McGuin, rpt. in *London Review of Books*, 23 Jan. 1986: 24–25.
8. *In Search of Immortality*, narrator Leonard Nemoy, The History Channel, 26 Jan. 2000.
9. A. U. Smith, *Biological Effects of Freezing and Supercooling* (Baltimore: Williams & Wilkins, 1961).
10. A. U. Smith, *Biological Effects of Freezing and Supercooling* (Baltimore: Williams & Wilkins, 1961).
11. J. E. Lovelock, "Diathermy Apparatus for the Rapid Rewarming of Whole Animals from 0°C and Below." *Proceedings of the Royal Society* 3, v. 147, 1957, p. 545.)
12. A. U. Smith, *Biological Effects of Freezing and Supercooling* (Baltimore: Williams & Wilkins, 1961).
13. J. R. Kenyon, J. Ludbrook, A. R. Downs, I. B. Tait, D. K. Brooks, and J. Pryczkowski, "Experimental Deep Hypothermia," *Lancet* ii (1959): 41.
14. D. K. C. MacDonald, *Near Zero: An Introduction to Low Temperature Physics* (New York: Doubleday & Co., 1961).
15. *Globe and Mail* 28 Jan. 2000.
16. T.D. Kvittingen and A. Nasse, "Recovery from Drowning in Fresh Water," *British Medical Journal* 18 May 1963.

17. Duncan MacDougal, *American Medicine* April 1907, rpt on http://www.artbell.com/duncan.html.

7

Evidence About Christ's Resurrection

> For I delivered unto you first of all that which I also received, how that Christ died for our sins according to the scriptures; And that he was buried, and that he rose again the third day according to the scriptures: And that he was seen of Cephas, then of the twelve. (1 Corinthians 15:3–5)

There is only one credible person in history who claims to have died and been resurrected from the dead several days later. That person, Jesus of Nazareth, died on the cross almost two thousand years ago. While many modern agnostic historians and even some theologians dispute the fact of Christ's resurrection, there is overwhelming historical and archeological evidence for its truth. As an examination of their writings reveal, the primary objection of critics of Jesus' resurrection stems from their prejudice against the supernatural. In fact, many of these critics philosophically reject the possibility that *any* supernatural miracle can occur. In this chapter we will examine the historical evidence for the resurrection of Jesus and answer the objections that have been raised by critics.

An anonymous Christian writer once wrote a statement about the significance of the doctrine of resurrection to the Christian faith. He wrote, "Christianity begins where religion ends . . . with the Resurrection." The unique promise of bodily resurrection is that we shall live again in our own renewed and immortal as well as incorruptible bodies. This is the extraordinary doctrine of resurrection that is central to Jesus Christ's teaching. The hope of our resurrection is the core of Christianity that forever transforms our spiritual life and all or our hopes for tomorrow.

The historical truth about the resurrection of Jesus Christ is the essential bedrock upon which the Christian faith rests. The claim of Christianity, that Jesus of Nazareth rose from the dead, is either the most important fact in human history or it is nothing less than an enormous hoax. If Jesus truly rose from the dead, His resurrection as the Son of God provides the greatest evidence that we ourselves will also rise from the dead in the last days. However, if Jesus' body is still in some undiscovered grave in Israel, then the claims of Christianity are fraudulent. The apostle Paul declares, "If Christ is not risen, then our preaching is empty" (1 Corinthians 15:14). If Jesus did not truly rise, victorious over death, then the promise of his sacrificial death atoning for our sins would be false; He would not be the sinless One whose death wins our pardon before the Throne of God. In fact, the apostle Paul declared that the unique resurrection of Jesus Christ provided God's strongest declaration that He was truly the Son of God. Paul wrote, "Concerning his Son Jesus Christ our Lord, which was made of the seed of David according to the flesh; And declared to be the Son of God with power, according to the spirit of holiness, by the resurrection from the dead" (Romans 1:3–4).

Jesus' resurrection was fundamental teaching of the early Church as demonstrated in the book of Acts where we find eight major sermons that teach that the doctrine of Christ's resurrection is the bedrock of Christian faith and belief. While most other religions are based on a complex philosophy of ideas, Christianity is based on the historical fact of Jesus Christ's resurrection. As one scholarly critic who personally rejects the truth of the resurrection acknowledged, "Indeed, without a belief in the Resurrection, Christianity as a religion would never have begun to exist."[1] Therefore, it is vital that we examine the historical and archeological evidence that points to Christ's resurrection from the Garden Tomb.

The apostle Paul, writing only thirty years after the event, said that Jesus' resurrection was confirmed by over five hundred eyewitnesses who he knew to be first-hand eyewitnesses of the resurrected Christ. He affirmed that most of these eyewitnesses were still alive when he wrote his epistle to the church at Corinth. Many liberal scholars now admit that the first three Gospel accounts of Matthew, Mark, and Luke regarding the life, death, and resurrection of Jesus were written and widely distributed within thirty-five to forty years of Jesus' death. Thousands of people who saw Jesus alive during the forty days following His resurrection, until His ascension to Heaven, were still alive to read these widely distributed documents. Moreover, there is absolutely no evidence from contemporary historical documents that any of these eyewitnesses disputed the Gospel accounts.

The apostle Paul wrote,

> But now is Christ risen from the dead, and become the firstfruits of them that slept. For since by man came death, by man came also the resurrection of the dead. For as in Adam all die, even so in Christ shall all be made alive. But every man in his own order: Christ the firstfruits; afterward they that are Christ's at his coming. (1 Corinthians 15:20–23)

Most scholars now generally agree that the three Synoptic Gospel accounts in Matthew, Mark, and Luke, which recount the life, death, and resurrection of Jesus, were written and widely distributed within thirty-five to forty years of the events recorded in the Gospels. The great British archeologist Sir William Ramsey initially set out to debunk the historical authority of the Gospel writers, but the overwhelming historical evidence he discovered convinced him to write a different book — a book that established powerful proof that the Gospels' account of the life, death, and resurrection of Jesus of Nazareth was authentic. He wrote, "Luke's history is unsurpassed in respect of its trustworthiness. . . . Luke is a historian of the first rank; not merely are his statements of fact trustworthy; he is possessed of the true historic sense. . . . In short, this historian should be placed along with the very greatest of historians."[2] Another great New Testament scholar, Professor F. F. Bruce, wrote, "Where Luke has been suspected of inaccuracy, and accuracy has been vindicated by some inscriptional evidence, it may be legitimate to say that archeology has confirmed the New Testament record."[3]

There is additional archeological and historical evidence

that Matthew, Mark, and Luke were written and widely distributed within three or four decades of the events they describe. These three gospels were distributed and read publicly in churches during the time when thousands of eyewitnesses who had personally witnessed miracles such as the feeding of the five thousand and had seen the risen Savior preaching after His death on the cross were still alive. In several previous books, *The Signature of God* and *Jesus: The Great Debate,* I explored some fascinating quotations from the Dead Sea Scrolls that appear to contain passages and verses from the Synoptic Gospels. Since the Dead Sea Scrolls were buried in caves in A.D. 68, this would support the case for the early writing of the Gospels. Furthermore, a well-respected Church historian, Professor Samuel H. Moffett, has written a brilliant analysis of the growth of the early Church in the East, entitled *A History of Christianity in Asia*.[4] In this book Moffett presents compelling evidence from early Christian manuscripts, including the brilliant scholar Pantaenus (A.D. 172) and the Church historian Eusebius (A.D. 260 to 33), that suggests that Bartholomew, a disciple of Jesus, took a copy of the gospel of Matthew in its original Hebrew manuscript form to India in approximately A.D. 52 to 60, only two decades after Christ's resurrection.

Thousands of people who saw the resurrected Jesus were still alive to read these widely distributed gospel documents about His resurrection. Paul wrote, "After that, he was seen of above five hundred brethren at once; of whom the greater part remain unto this present, but some are fallen asleep" (1 Corinthians 15:6). There is no historical record that even one of these hundreds of eyewitnesses disputed the facts of Christ's physical resurrection from the tomb. In fact, the Greek historian Thallus records the supernatural eclipse that occurred when the heavens were darkened at the crucifixion of Jesus during Passover in the year A.D. 32.

Death by crucifixion was the most terrible of all methods of execution devised by ancient conquerors. The Persians and Carthoginians first developed this horrifying practice around 600 B.C. Alexander the Great crucified two thousand citizens of the conquered city of Tyre after the city finally surrendered to his Macedonian legions on the eastern shore of the Mediterranean Sea. The Romans subsequently adopted this execution technique to terrorize their enemies, beginning with the Roman general Crassus' crucifixion of thousands of recaptured slaves who had revolted under the leadership of Spartacus. Later, Caesar Augustus introduced crucifixion as a general policy and crucified over six thousand rebellious slaves in Sicily during the war against Sextus Pompeius. Quintillian, a Roman author, wrote about the Roman government's motivation for crucifying their enemies. "Whenever we crucify criminals, very crowded highways are chosen so that many may see it and many may be moved by fear of it; because all punishment does not pertain as much to revenge as to example." The Roman philosopher Cicero was so appalled by crucifixion that he warned that Roman citizens should not be exposed to the sights or sounds of victims suffering crucifixion. Cicero declared that crucifixion was "the most cruel and hideous of tortures."[5]

In fact, Roman law decreed that crucifixion could not be used to punish its citizens, only its foreign enemies. Roman citizens were normally beheaded in capital cases.[6] This is the reason the apostle Paul, a free Roman citizen, was beheaded, while the apostle Peter and other Christians died on crosses. Just a few years before the trial of Christ, Rome tightened its grip on the levers of political and judicial life in the increasingly rebellious Israel by eliminating the Jews' independent legal authority to declare death sentences for any crimes. That is why the Jewish priests of the Sanhedrin court were forced to appeal to the Roman authority of Governor Pontius Pilate and accuse Jesus of crimes against Rome in order to secure a sentence of death by crucifixion.

Did Jesus Actually Die on the Cross?

One of the first issues to be examined is one raised by some critics who question whether or not Jesus really died on the cross. They suggest that He somehow survived the brutal whipping, the crown of thorns, the spikes through His wrists and feet, and the spear thrust through his side. To lend support to their theory, they point out the surprise expressed by Pontius Pilate, the Roman governor, to the unusually swift death of Jesus. The disciple Mark wrote:

> Joseph of Arimathaea, an honourable counsellor, which also waited for the kingdom of God, came, and went in boldly unto Pilate, and craved the body of Jesus. And Pilate marvelled if he were already dead: and calling unto him the centurion, he asked him whether he had been any while dead. And when he knew it of the centurion, he gave the body to Joseph. (Mark 15:42–45)

However, when we carefully examine this Gospel record, we discover that the Roman centurion was specifically asked by Pontius Pilate to verify the death of Jesus. Centurions were exceedingly familiar with the physical signs of death from warfare and the multitude of executions over which they presided. In this case, the centurion himself thrust the spear through the body of Christ on the cross to verify that death had occurred. It would have probably cost him his life had he verified to a Roman governor that a condemned prisoner was dead if, in fact, he was still alive.

> But when they came to Jesus, and saw that he was dead already, they brake not his legs: But one of the soldiers with a spear pierced his side, and forthwith came there out blood and water. And he that saw it bare record, and his record is true: and he knoweth that he saith true, that ye might believe. (John 19:33–35)

The fact that the centurion was not executed following the widely discussed reports of Christ's resurrection provides strong proof that the Jewish and Roman authorities accepted the fact of Christ's death. Various medical doctors who have examined the description of the horrible scourging suggest that punishment alone could have killed Jesus. The early Christian historian Eusebius recorded the fate of those exposed to Roman scourging. "The sufferer's veins were laid bare, and the very muscles, sinews, and bowels of the victim were open to exposure."[7] The account of Jesus' crucifixion includes the fact that "blood and water" poured forth from His chest. This fact is evidence that Jesus was already dead when the spear pierced His side. Dr. Truman Davis wrote that there was "an escape of watery fluid from the sac surrounding the heart. We, therefore, have rather conclusive postmortem evidence that he died, not the usual crucifixion death by suffocation, but of heart failure due to shock and constriction of the heart by fluid in the pericardium."[8]

Critics point to one known case where an individual who was crucified and later removed from the cross subsequently survived. Josephus Flavius, the Jewish historian, gives an account of three of his friends who were hung on crosses but taken down when he appealed to the Roman general Titus for mercy. Despite being immediately taken down from their crosses, only one of the three was able to survive, even with medical assistance. However, to put this in context, Jesus was not only scourged unmercifully, crowned with brutally sharp thorns, and hung on the cross for many hours, but a centurion thrust a spear through his chest to verify His death before allowing burial. Jesus' body was then placed in a cold rock tomb and left for several days.

A great skeptic of the Resurrection, David F. Strauss, admits that the claim that Jesus swooned and recovered consciousness in the cold tomb was untenable. Strauss wrote,

> It is impossible that a being who had stolen half-dead out of the sepulchre, who crept about weak and ill, wanting medical treatment, who required bandaging, strengthening and indulgence, and who still at least yielded to his sufferings, could have given to the disciples the impression that he was a Conqueror over death and the grave, the Prince of Life, an impression which lay at the bottom of their future ministry. Such a resuscitation could only have weakened the impression which He had made upon them in life and in death, at the most could only have given it an elegiac voice, but could by no possibility have changed their sorrow into enthusiasm, have elevated their reverence into worship.[9]

Significantly, there were a variety of eyewitnesses who attested to the physical death of Jesus. These eyewitnesses to His death include the centurion, the various soldiers who participated in the crucifixion, Joseph of Arimathaea and Nicodemus, who buried the body in the tomb, and the women "Mary Magdalene, and the other Mary sitting over against the sepulchre" (Matthew 27:61). The evidence is sound; Jesus truly died on the cross. Significantly, not one of the enemies of the Church in the first century ever attempted to claim that Jesus didn't die. The Gospel accounts about Jesus' death on the cross can pass the historical test for authenticity.

Historical Evidence of a Miracle at Jesus's Crucifixion

When we examine the historical reliability of an event, especially a remarkable, miraculous, and absolutely unique event such as the claim that Jesus actually rose from the dead, any historical confirmation of other related events that occurred at the same time adds legitimacy to the historical truth of the account. For example, the Israeli archeologist's discovery in 1991 of the ancient tomb of Josephus Caiaphas, the High Priest who presided over the trial of Jesus, provides additional support for the truthfulness of the Gospel account.

Additionally, independent, contemporary historical documents from non-Christian sources confirm that a supernatural miracle occurred during the same hours as Jesus' crucifixion. I am referring to the astonishing claim in the Gospels of Matthew, Mark, and Luke that God supernaturally darkened the sky over the earth for three hours during the time when His Son Jesus Christ hung on the cross. This miraculous darkness was a powerful and supernatural sign to all eyewitnesses that God had intervened to demonstrate His divine power. Significantly, over six centuries earlier, the Old Testament prophet Amos had predicted precisely such an event would occur:

And it shall come to pass in that day, saith the Lord

> God, that I will cause the sun to go down at noon, and I will darken the earth in the clear day: And I will turn your feasts into mourning, and all your songs into lamentation; and I will bring up sackcloth upon all loins, and baldness upon every head; and I will make it as the mourning of an only son, and the end thereof as a bitter day. (Amos 8:9–10)

Note that the prophet Amos predicted that the following miraculous events would occur in the future concerning God's "only son":

1) *Darkness at noon*: "I will cause the sun to go down at noon, and I will darken the earth in the clear day"
2) *A Feast Day*: "I will turn your feasts into mourning"
3) *It will lead to mourning for death of an only son*: "I will make it as the mourning of an only son."

There are five independent eyewitness historical records of this remarkable event including Matthew, Mark, Luke, and two non-Christian pagan historians, Thallus and Phlegon. For example, Matthew wrote, "Now from the sixth hour there was darkness over all the land unto the ninth hour" (Matthew 27:45). Mark recorded the following, "And when the sixth hour was come, there was darkness over the whole land until the ninth hour" (Mark 15:33). Finally, Luke declared, "And it was about the sixth hour, and there was a darkness over all the earth until the ninth hour. And the sun was darkened, and the veil of the temple was rent in the midst"(Luke 23:44–45).

Consider the implications of these statements. If this astonishing miracle of darkness in the middle of the day for three hours did not actually occur, then Christianity would have died at its birth because it would have become the laughingstock of the Roman empire. To claim falsely that one of the most remarkable events that any group of people could ever experience — total darkness at noon on Passover A.D. 32 — had occurred, if in fact, it did *not* occur, would have caused everyone to dismiss the new religion. However, there are no historical references to any Jewish or Gentile critic attacking the veracity of the Gospel accounts about Jesus' death by ridiculing the claim that this powerful miracle occurred on that same day. Both the Romans and the Jewish people knew very well that this mid-day three-hour darkness could not have been the result of an eclipse of the sun because the Feast of Passover always occurred precisely at the time of the full moon. Any astronomer can confirm that an eclipse of the sun is impossible during the time of a full moon, due to the position of the sun, moon, and earth.

Only twenty years after the death of Christ, the pagan Greek historian Thallus records in his *Third History,* written in A.D. 52, that the heavens were darkened throughout the known world during the time of Passover in the year A.D. 32 when the crucifixion of Jesus occurred. Another contemporary Greek pagan historian, Phlegon, confirmed that this unusual darkness lasted precisely three hours from noon to exactly three o'clock. Phlegon wrote, "During the time of Tiberius Caesar an eclipse of the sun occurred during the full moon."[10] Another ancient writer, Philopon, wrote, "Phlegon mentioned the eclipse which took place during the crucifixion of the Lord Jesus Christ, and no other, it is clear that he did not know from his sources about any eclipse in previous times . . . and this is shown by the historical account itself of Tiberius Caesar."[11] Both of these accounts confirm the Gospel narratives.

A well-respected early Christian historian (A.D. 221),

Julius Africanus, also wrote about this supernatural darkness:

> As to [Jesus'] works . . . and the resurrection from the dead, these have been most authoritatively set forth by His disciples and apostles before us. On the whole world there pressed a most fearful darkness; and the rocks were rent by an earthquake, and many places in Judea and other districts were thrown down. This darkness, Thallus, in the third book of his *History*, calls as appears to me without reason, an eclipse of the sun. For the Hebrews celebrate the passover on the 14th day according to the moon, and the passion of our Savior falls on the day before the passover; but an eclipse of the sun takes place only when the moon comes under the sun."[12]

There is far more historically verifiable evidence that Jesus Christ lived, died, and rose from the dead than exists to prove many of the historical statements about events and personalities in ancient history. Although God calls us to walk in faith, He also provides reasonable evidence, both historical and scientific, to assure us that our faith is built on truthful and accurate accounts of the life, death, and resurrection of Jesus of Nazareth.

Historical Evidence About Christ's Resurrection

The New Testament claims that Jesus of Nazareth died and then rose from His grave on the third day to triumph over death and the grave. If this event can be proven actually to have occurred, then the further claims of the New Testament regarding Jesus Christ's descriptions about life after death should be considered authoritative. In the balance of this chapter we will examine the evidence regarding His death and resurrection to determine if it is authentic.

There are seven primary first-century historical documents that provide contemporary evidence that the resurrection of Jesus was an historical event. These documents include the writings of Paul, Matthew, Mark, Luke, John, Peter, and Flavius Josephus. The earliest historical reference to the resurrection is found in a letter from the apostle Paul to the church at Corinth. In it he describes that Christ made several appearances to people after He arose from the dead. The majority of scholars agree that this letter was written by Paul in A.D. 56, within twenty-four years of Christ's resurrection.

> For I delivered unto you first of all that which I also received, how that Christ died for our sins according to the scriptures; And that he was buried, and that he rose again the third day according to the scriptures: And that he was seen of Cephas, then of the twelve: After that, he was seen of above five hundred brethren at once; of whom the greater part remain unto this present, but some are fallen asleep. After that, he was seen of James; then of all the apostles. (1 Corinthians 15:3–7)

The disciples Matthew, Mark, and Luke also recorded the resurrection from their own eyewitness experiences within the first forty years of the event. Although the disciple John wrote his gospel after the others, most New Testament scholars acknowledge that he produced his account of the resurrection by approximately A.D. 85, only fifty-three years after the event. The disciple Peter confirmed the resurrection account in his ministry and declared that he was an eyewitness to the historical events he recorded in his epistle. "For we have not followed cunningly devised fables, when we made known unto you the power and coming of our Lord Jesus Christ, but were eyewitnesses of his majesty" (2 Peter 1:16). In the book of Acts, Luke states that Peter witnessed the death of Jesus on the cross and His activities after His resurrection. Peter acknowledged that he had shared meals with Jesus during the forty days between the Resurrection and Christ's ascension to Heaven. Peter declared, "And we are witnesses of all things which he did both in the land of the Jews, and in Jerusalem; whom they slew and hanged on a tree: Him God raised up the third day, and showed him openly; Not to all the people, but unto witnesses chosen before of God, even to us, who did eat and drink with him after he rose from the dead" (Acts 10:39–41).

The Reports of Jesus' Appearances Following His Resurrection

If Jesus Christ had only appeared to one or two disciples after his resurrection, it would be easy to imagine that the evidence was not strong enough to support the claims of Christianity. However, as evidence from the New Testament will amply demonstrate, Jesus of Nazareth appeared in His resurrection body many times over a period of forty days to a wide variety of witnesses in a large number of locations.

The Gospels record a number of occasions in which Jesus appeared in the flesh to many people following His resurrection, during the six-week period between the festival of Passover and the festival of Firstfruits. The specific resurrection appearances of Jesus that are detailed in the New Testament are listed below:

1) He appeared to Mary Magdalene early on Sunday outside the sepulchre (John 20:11–18; Mark 16:9).
"Mary Magdalene came and told the disciples that she had seen the Lord, and that he had spoken these things unto her" (John 20:18).
2) Jesus appeared to another female follower named Mary (Matthew 28:1, 8–10).
"In the end of the sabbath, as it began to dawn toward the first day of the week, came Mary Magdalene and the other Mary to see the sepulchre . . . behold, Jesus met them, saying, All hail. And they came and held him by the feet, and worshipped him" (Matthew 28:1, 9).
3) He appeared to Peter and the other disciples (Luke 24:34, 1 Corinthians 15:5).
"Saying, The Lord is risen indeed, and hath appeared to Simon" (Luke 24:34).
4) Christ met an unknown disciple and the uncle of Jesus, Cleopas, on the road to Emmaus (Luke 24:13–35).
5) He appeared to ten of His disciples at one time (Luke 24:36–43).
"And as they thus spake, Jesus himself stood in the midst of them, and saith unto them, Peace be unto you" (Luke 24:36).
6) Eight days later Jesus appeared to all His eleven disciples (John 20:24–29).
"But Thomas, one of the twelve, called Didymus, was not with them when Jesus came.
The other disciples therefore said unto him, We have seen the Lord" (John 20:24–25).
7) Jesus met seven of His disciples on the shore of the Sea of Galilee (John 21:1–23).
"After these things Jesus showed himself again to the disciples at the sea of Tiberias; and on this wise

showed he himself. There were together Simon Peter, and Thomas called Didymus, and Nathanael of Cana in Galilee, and the sons of Zebedee, and two other of his disciples" (John 21:1–2).

8) Christ appeared to five hundred witnesses, most of whom, according to Paul, were still alive at the time he wrote his letter to the church in Corinth (1 Corinthians 15:6).
   "After that, he was seen of above five hundred brethren at once; of whom the greater part remain unto this present, but some are fallen asleep" (I Corinthians 15:6).
9) He appeared to His brother James and then to all of his disciples (I Corinthians 15:7).
   "After that, he was seen of James; then of all the apostles" (1 Corinthians 15:7).
10) Jesus ascended to Heaven in the sight of His eleven disciples on the Mount of Olives (Acts 1:3–12).
   "To whom also he showed himself alive after his passion by many infallible proofs, being seen of them forty days, and speaking of the things pertaining to the kingdom of God. And when he had spoken these things, while they beheld, he was taken up; and a cloud received him out of their sight" (Acts 1:3, 9).

When we examine all of these post-resurrection appearances to hundreds of people who had known Jesus personally for years, the evidence is unmistakable that these witnesses saw Jesus in the flesh and personally attested to many others that they were convinced of the reality they saw — Jesus was physically resurrected from the dead. Many of these witnesses, including the eleven disciples, faced terrible persecution, including martyrdom, rather than deny their faith in the resurrection of Jesus Christ.

The Empty Tomb

The most obvious fact about the resurrection of Jesus is that His tomb was empty. This fact is attested to by the team of guards, the Jewish chief priests who bribed those guards, the women followers of Jesus who came to the tomb, and the disciples who also visited the empty tomb.

Both the Roman authorities as well as the Jewish high priests had the strongest possible motive to prove that the resurrection of Jesus of Nazareth had not occurred. All they had to do to effectively destroy the claims of Christ's disciples about His resurrection and to cut the foundation out from under the new religion was to produce the body. With all of the coercive power of Roman threats and monetary rewards offered by the Jewish high priests, it is extremely improbable that someone would not have been able to find the body of Jesus had it been reburied anywhere in Israel.

For example, the great Jewish teacher and leader of the Sanhedrin, Rabbi Gamaliel, warned his fellow sages that they should refrain from persecuting the followers of Jesus Christ, just in case God was, in fact, supporting their religious movement and revelation. The disciple Luke recorded the following:

> Then stood there up one in the council, a Pharisee, named Gamaliel, a doctor of the law, had in reputation among all the people, and commanded to put the apostles forth a little space; And said unto them, Ye men of Israel, take heed to yourselves what ye intend to do as touching these men . . . And now I

> say unto you, Refrain from these men, and let them alone: for if this counsel or this work be of men, it will come to nought: But if it be of God, ye cannot overthrow it; lest haply ye be found even to fight against God. And to him they agreed: and when they had called the apostles, and beaten them, they commanded that they should not speak in the name of Jesus, and let them go. (Acts 5:34,35,38–40)

Why would the great Jewish sage Gamaliel or his colleagues have responded this way if they had the slightest doubt that the tomb that once held the body of Jesus was now empty?

It is very significant that Christianity did not originate and grow in some obscure outpost of the Roman empire. The historical truth is that Christianity began and flourished during the first century in Jerusalem and throughout Israel, where tens of thousands of individuals still lived who were alive when miracles such as the feeding of the five thousand and the resurrection appearances of Jesus Christ occurred. If these events had not occurred as they were described in the Gospels, the negative reaction of the population to such invented claims would have quickly destroyed Christianity. The acknowledged fact of the empty tomb could not be denied by any objective historian who analyzed the evidence. The brilliant scholar Arthur Ramsey wrote, "I believe in the resurrection, partly because a series of facts are unaccountable without it." Ramsey stated that the undeniable fact of the empty tomb was "too notorious to be denied."[13]

Evidence from the Jewish Historian Flavius Josephus

Flavius Josephus was the greatest Jewish historian of the first century. He provided us with the most authoritative account of the historical events that occurred in Israel during the first century. It is no exaggeration to state that Flavius Josephus is considered to be the major historical source for the events during this period in Palestine, apart from the accounts in the New Testament. Although Jewish scholars despise him for his abandonment of the Jewish rebellion against Rome, and for joining their enemies and living as a friend of the Roman Emperor Vespasian in Italy, they admit that he is often our sole reliable source for the events that occurred during that tumultuous century. In light of the acknowledged fact that Jesus of Nazareth did live and die during these decades it is not surprising that Josephus chose to mention Jesus of Nazareth in his historical writings, entitled *Antiquities of the Jews*.

> Now there was about this time Jesus, a wise man, if it be lawful to call him a man, for he was a doer of wonderful works, a teacher of such doer of wonderful works, a teacher of such men as receive the truth with pleasure. He drew over to him both many of the Jews, and many of the Gentiles. He was [the] Christ, and when Pilate, at the suggestion of the principal men among us, had condemned him to the cross, those that loved him at the first did not forsake him: for he appeared to them alive again the third day: as the divine prophets had foretold these and ten thousand other wonderful things concerning him. And the tribe of Christians so named from him are not extinct at this day"[14]

Flavius Josephus lived as a priest and a member of the Pharisee party in Jerusalem. Born in A.D. 37, only a few years after the death of Christ, Josephus witnessed the political events leading up to the destruction of Jerusalem and the Temple. After serving as a general of the Jewish rebel army in Galilee during the war of independence against Rome, Josephus was captured by the Romans when the city of Jotapata fell. Later, he became friends with the Roman general Vespasian, who became emperor of Rome. As a historian, with access to official Roman and Jewish governmental archives and historical records, Josephus wrote about the chaotic events in Israel during the first century of this era. Josephus published his definitive study of the history of the Jewish people, *Antiquities of the Jews,* in A.D. 94.

Many liberal scholars have suggested that Josephus' reference to Jesus Christ might be interpolations or forgeries by later Christian editors. They suggest that Josephus' reference to Jesus was not authentic. An assertion of historical forgery demands significant proof. However, no scholars have produced any ancient copy of *Antiquities of the Jew*s that does not include this passage on Jesus. Phillip Schaff declared in his book, *History of the Christian Church,* that every existing ancient copy of Josephus' book, including the early Slavonic (Russian) and Arabic language versions, contain the disputed passage about the death and resurrection of Jesus Christ. In addition, no one has ever successfully explained how anyone could have altered each of these widely distributed editions in the centuries following their original publication. Prejudice is the fundamental reason why critics reject Josephus' reference to Christ. It is only natural that Josephus would mention the historical events concerning Christ at the appropriate place in his narrative of that turbulent century. In reality, if Josephus failed to mention the well-known ministry and resurrection of Jesus of Nazareth, it would be more curious.

In 1987, the biblical scholar Craig Blomberg, author of *The Historical Reliability of the Gospels,* stated that "many recent studies of Josephus however, agree that much of the passage closely resembles Josephus' style of writing elsewhere. . . . But most of the passage seems to be authentic and is certainly the most important ancient non-Christian testimony to the life of Jesus which has been preserved." Blomberg concluded his lengthy analysis with this statement "The gospels may therefore be trusted as historically reliable."

Professor R. C. Stone also wrote a scholarly article on this subject, entitled "Josephus," in which he said, "The passage concerning Jesus has been regarded by some as a Christian interpolation; but the bulk of the evidence, both external and internal, marks it as genuine. Josephus must have known the main facts about the life and death of Jesus, and his historian's curiosity certainly would lead him to investigate the movement which was gaining adherents even in high circles. Arnold Toynbee rates him among the five greatest Hellenic historians."[15]

Did the Disciples Steal His Body?

The claim that the disciples stole the body of Jesus was first made by the Jewish priests, who were dismayed at the reports that Christ had risen from the dead and that His body was no longer to be found in the tomb. Matthew recorded this vain attempt to account for the missing body.

Now when they were going, behold, some of the

> watch came into the city, and showed unto the chief priests all the things that were done. And when they were assembled with the elders, and had taken counsel, they gave large money unto the soldiers, Saying, Say ye, His disciples came by night, and stole him away while we slept. And if this come to the governor's ears, we will persuade him, and secure you. So they took the money, and did as they were taught: and this saying is commonly reported among the Jews until this day. (Matthew 28:11–15)

Recently, some agnostic critics have resurrected this ancient claim by suggesting that some of Christ's disciples came back to the tomb to steal Jesus' body, in order to secretly rebury it so that no one would ever be able to deny His claimed resurrection. There is no question that the guard unit included many soldiers. Matthew stated that "some of the watch" attempted to excuse themselves for failing to prevent the disappearance of Christ's body: "Now when they were going, behold, some of the watch came into the city, and showed unto the chief priests all the things that were done" (Matthew 28:11). A key point to remember is that the claim by the Jewish authorities that the disciples had stolen the body of Jesus is the strongest possible proof that the tomb was empty. Any lawyer will tell you that the admission of a key fact by your enemies is the conclusive evidence that the fact in question is true.

There is an argument among scholars about whether the tomb guard unit was composed of Roman soldiers or a special unit of Jewish Temple guards. If it was a Jewish guard unit, it would have been composed of ten specially trained Levites who were pledged to protect religious places under the threat of severe punishment if they fell asleep on duty. The rules of discipline for Jewish Temple guards were so severe that if anyone fell asleep at their post, the chief guard was authorized to beat them and set their clothes on fire. The suggestion that all ten of such well-trained and disciplined guards would allow themselves to fall asleep at the same time is obviously unreasonable.

The other possibility, and the more probable of the two, is that the guard unit was composed of regular Roman troops from the legion stationed at Jerusalem. A well-respected New Testament Greek scholar, Professor A. T. Robertson, declared that the Greek words translated "have a guard" must refer to the custodial guard unit of the Roman legion, which was notorious for its severe discipline. These sentry units of up to sixteen Roman soldiers served under extreme discipline, which called for execution if a sentry fell asleep at his post. These brutal rules condemned to death anyone who deserted their night watch, or anyone who was guilty of "falling asleep." If it could not be determined who fell asleep and endangered his fellow troops, they would draw lots and burn to death the unlucky soldier who drew the designated lot, as an inducement to keep faith with their fellow soldiers on night watch.

The Roman guards placed a special official cord across the rolled stone, securing the tomb with sealing clay on both sides, to ensure the integrity of the grave against any potential grave robbers. The placement of this cord and its affixed clay seal on the tomb was a sign to everyone that the authority of Roman law would condemn them if they violated the sanctity of this grave.[16] Roman law demanded that anyone who violated a Roman seal be crucified upside-down. Matthew reported, "So they went, and made the sepulchre sure, sealing the stone, and setting a watch" (Matthew 27:66). Anyone who violated a place that was sealed under the legal authority of Rome was sentenced to death. That is why the Roman soldiers requested that the Jewish chief priests intervene on their behalf to persuade the Roman governor not to punish them for their failure to prevent the disappearance of Christ's body. If the tomb wasn't empty, why would the soldiers leave the tomb they were guarding to go report to the Jewish religious authorities?

Aside from the other objections mentioned above, the attitude of Christ's disciples was not one that would have motivated them to dare to steal the body of their crucified leader from under the vigilant guard of the authorities. The disciples, at that time, had been so fearful of being apprehended by the Roman or Jewish authorities that they were hiding. Furthermore, Christ's disciples so lacked faith in His resurrection from the grave that they didn't even believe the initial reports of the women who saw the empty tomb.

Did the Roman or Jewish Authorities Take the Body?

Other critics suggest alternatively that Roman or Jewish authorities secretly removed Christ's body. This scenario is equally untenable. Neither the Roman officials nor the Jewish authorities had any conceivable reason to hide His body. If the Roman or Jewish authorities had the slightest idea where they could locate the body of Jesus, they would have produced His corpse and destroyed the new faith before it had a chance to grow.

Did the Women Go to the Wrong Tomb?

More recently, several critics have suggested that the women simply had gotten lost and had gone to the wrong tomb. The women then told the male disciples of Jesus that their

Messiah had disappeared, thus creating the myth of His resurrection.

This extraordinary suggestion is without serious merit. The Gospel record tells us that several of the women followers of Christ who visited the tomb on Sunday morning were the same women who were present at the tomb when Joseph of Arimathaea and Nicodemus prepared the body of Christ with spices and buried their Master. Matthew wrote that the two women who were present at the burial were also present on Sunday morning when the tomb was discovered to be empty, "And there was Mary Magdalene, and the other Mary, sitting over against the sepulchre" (Matthew 27:61). The Gospels clearly reveal that the tomb in which Jesus was buried was very near the place of His execution, known as Golgotha. "Now in the place where he was crucified there was a garden; and in the garden a new sepulchre, wherein was never man yet laid" (John 19:41). These women were present at the crucifixion of Jesus and immediately followed Joseph and Arimathaea and Nicodemus as they carried the body of Christ from Golgotha to the nearby tomb, which was owned by their friend Joseph. The suggestion that the women could have failed to remember the directions to the tomb, which was on the grounds of the property of their friend Joseph of Arimathaea, and close by the place of execution, is illogical. Even if this ridiculous suggestion was correct, the women would have immediately inquired about the correct location from its owner, Joseph of Arimaethia, or his friend, Nicodemus.

Did the Disciples Suffer from Hallucinations?

One final suggestion to account for the belief in the Resurrection is that the disciples and followers of Jesus suffered from delusion. They falsely believed that Jesus had risen from the tomb and that they had seen him alive during the forty days before His ascension to Heaven. In considering this possibility, it is important to remember the essential qualification of those who were accredited as "apostles" of the Lord. When Judas Iscariot betrayed the Lord and committed suicide, the remaining disciples felt the need to replace him with another disciple to make up "the Twelve." However, the qualification of Matthias as the replacement disciple of Christ was that he had to be able to testify as an eyewitness of the key events in the life, death, and resurrection of Jesus (Acts 1:21-26). The absurd claim of agnostics that hundreds of individuals of widely different backgrounds and psychological temperments would succumb, for forty days, to a single hallucination that Jesus rose from the dead is contradicted by everything we know about hallucinations. Psychologists affirm that hallucinations are subjective to the individual, not shared with others. Moreover, hallucinations usually are experienced by individuals who are highly nervous and very imaginative. The famous neurobiologist, Professor R. Mourgue, wrote a study on hallucinations in which he explains that these subjective psychological phenomena are almost always characterized by variability and inconstancy.[17]

However, the New Testament records reveal that hundreds of individuals of widely different temperment, over many weeks, and in a multitude of locations, recognized and affirmed publicly that Jesus had truly risen, triumphant over death despite their absolute knowledge that he had died in agony on the cross. This view is expressed also by Thomas James Thorburn:

It is absolutely inconceivable that as many as five

> hundred persons, of average soundness of mind and temperment, in various numbers, at all sorts of times, and in divers situations, should experience all kinds of sensuous impressions — visual, auditory, factual — and that all these manifold experiences should rest entirely upon subjective hallucination. We say that this is incredible, because if such a theory were applied to any other than a 'supernatural' event in history, it would be dismissed forthwith as a ridiculously insufficient explanation.[18]

There is no other example in history of a diverse group of people experiencing a common hallucination, which they continue to affirm against great opposition for many years. In conclusion, the suggestion that the followers of Jesus suffered from a hallucination is without foundation and must be rejected.

Who Rolled the Stone Away?

Another major problem with the theory that the disciples somehow removed the body of Jesus from under the guard of the soldiers is that the enormous rounded stone used to close such tombs was rolled down an incline in order to seal the tomb's entrance. It is significant that each of the four Gospel writers mentions the stone. During a number of research trips to Israel, I spoke with archeologists and personally examined several tombs that contained rolled stones, such as the tomb of the family of King Herod and the Garden Tomb. In every case it would have taken extraordinary efforts to remove the stone once it had been rolled into position. The design of the tomb purposely made it very difficult for anyone, such as grave robbers, to easily open the tomb once the stone had been rolled into position to close the tomb entrance.

The doorway of the Garden Tomb, which may be the actual tomb of Jesus, has an indented groove that runs parallel to the cliff face into which the tomb was carved. A rolled stone sufficiently large enough to fit in this grove and to seal the entrance to this tomb would have weighed between one and two tons. The evidence from other tombs in Israel that appear to have utilized rolled stones to seal their entrances suggests that their rolled stones would also have weighed in excess of one ton. Each of the four Gospels refers to the massive size of this stone. The disciple Matthew wrote about Joseph of Arimathea, "And laid it in his own new tomb, which he had hewn out in the rock: and he rolled a great stone to the door of the sepulchre, and departed" (Matthew 27:60).

Therefore, it would have been exceedingly difficult, if not virtually impossible, for a small group of men to roll away such a huge stone back up an incline against the force of gravity, especially in darkness and if they were attempting to escape the notice of vigilant guards. A close examination of the historical evidence proves that there was something supernatural about the removal of the stone. Obviously, the Jewish authorities would have either personally, or by way of investigators, examined the site of the empty tomb after the event. The position of the huge stone that had been "rolled away" obviously must have indicated that there was no credible human explanation for its movement. The disciple Mark wrote that "when they looked, they saw that the stone was rolled away: for it was very great" (Mark 16:4). The Jewish authorities never would have accepted the testimony of the guards that they could not prevent the disappearance of Christ's body from the grave, except for the fact that the "great stone" could not possibly have been removed through natural means by Christ's disciples. In addition, we need to remember that these disciples were at the time disillusioned, disappointed, and depressed at the prospects of their imminent arrest and execution on the cross. To suggest that this group of frightened men would have endangered their lives to steal the dead body of Jesus away from armed guards when they themselves did not believe in His resurrection is simply not credible.

Old Testament Prophecies of the Resurrection

Throughout His ministry, Jesus repeatedly foretold that He would be killed and would rise again on the third day. Matthew records this prophecy: "From that time forth began Jesus to show unto his disciples, how that he must go unto Jerusalem, and suffer many things of the elders and chief priests and scribes, and be killed, and be raised again the third day" (Matthew 16:21). Moreover, Jesus affirmed that His resurrection from the grave was foretold in the prophecies of the Old Testament. On the road to Emmaus, Christ told His disciples, "O fools, and slow of heart to believe all that the prophets have spoken: Ought not Christ to have suffered these things, and to enter into his glory? And beginning at Moses and all the prophets, he expounded unto them in all the scriptures the things concerning himself" (Luke 24:25–27).

The Old Testament contains a number of prophecies that deal with the resurrection of the Messiah. In the Psalms, King David wrote the following prophecy:

> For thou wilt not leave my soul in [Sheol] Hell; neither wilt thou suffer thine Holy One to see corruption. Thou wilt show me the path of life: in thy

> presence is fullness of joy; at thy right hand there are pleasures for evermore. (Psalms 16:10–11)

This prophecy declared that God would deliver the Messiah from sheol and that He would deliver His Holy One from death and from enduring the "corruption" of the grave that every other body in history has experienced. In the New Testament both Paul and Peter refer to David's prophecy as a prediction of the resurrection of Jesus of Nazareth. In addition the Psalms contain other prophecies that refer to the Resurrection. David wrote of the future Messiah, "But God will redeem my soul from the power of the grave: for he shall receive me. Selah" (Psalms 49:15).

One of the most interesting Old Testament prophecies about the Messiah is found in the book of the prophet Hosea, who wrote, "Come, and let us return unto the Lord: for he hath torn, and he will heal us; he hath smitten, and he will bind us up. After two days will he revive us: in the third day he will raise us up, and we shall live in his sight" (Hosea 6:1–2). While this prophecy also refers to the resurrection of the nation of Israel, its language appears to refer to the resurrection of the Messiah "in the third day."

More directly, the prophet Isaiah's prophecy of the Suffering Servant also refers to the Resurrection: "Yet it pleased the Lord to bruise him; he hath put him to grief: when thou shalt make his soul an offering for sin, he shall see his seed, he shall prolong his days, and the pleasure of the Lord shall prosper in his hand" (Isaiah 53:10). The curious language of Isaiah 53 clearly predicts the Messiah's death as "an offering for sin" and then refers to the fact that, after his death, "he shall see his seed, he shall prolong his days, and the pleasure of the Lord shall prosper in his hand." Whatever else is involved in Isaiah's prophecy it is clear that the prophet is describing the resurrection of the Messiah to "prolong his days" and that he will "prosper."

The final Old Testament prophecy that clearly predicts the Resurrection is found in the book of Zechariah and was quoted by Jesus' beloved disciple: "And again another scripture saith, They shall look on him whom they pierced" (John 19:37). The prophet Zechariah predicted the crucifixion and the resurrection of the Messiah over five centuries before Jesus was born: "And I will pour upon the house of David, and upon the inhabitants of Jerusalem, the spirit of grace and of supplications: and they shall look upon me whom they have pierced, and they shall mourn for him, as one mourneth for his only son, and shall be in bitterness for him, as one that is in bitterness for his firstborn" (Zechariah 12:10). Logically, the only way anyone can "look upon me whom they have pierced" and "mourn for him, as one mourneth for his only son" is if the one who was pierced, the Messiah, was resurrected from death.

The introduction of Jesus Christ into our world transformed forever the way men relate to Heaven. His supernatural life, teaching, death, and resurrection revolutionized humanity's understanding and appreciation of the possibility of life after death. "In him was life; and the life was the light of men" (John 1:4).

Believers in Christ who sit in a hospital room with a dying Christian are filled with hope, not fear. We should not desire to hold our fellow Christian back from passing over the river to find Christ, peace, and eternal joy. Knowing that our friend's work on earth is finished, we can rejoice that the moment of death is also the moment our friend will pass into that eternal inheritance in Heaven above. When he breathes his last breath, our companion is not lost. He is truly found. His life, his mind, and his eternal spirit are now released to enjoy, without earthly limitations, all that Christ has prepared for those that love Him. This is not to say that we will not be sorrowful to lose a friend, yet this sorrow is comforted with the knowledge that our friend is going to a better place. Why should Christians mourn for departed loved ones as those who have no hope in death? Our friend's spirit and mind shall not enter the grave; only his body will rest temporarily there until the glorious moment of his resurrection, along with all of the departed saints.

The great secret of walking with Jesus Christ in faith is to accept fully His promises and teachings regarding His death for our sins, His resurrection from the grave, and His defeat of sin and the grave. His victory becomes ours when we enter into the promise of the coming resurrection through faith in Christ. In addition, our faith is focused on the future life that we will experience forever with Him in Heaven. While we cannot at this time see the fulfilment of His great promises about the heavenly city, the New Jerusalem, that glorious day will finally come. The tremendous promise of "a better country" in the presence of God motivated generations of ancient Jewish patriarchs and the faithful Christian martyrs that followed them to offer their lives and their bodies as martyrs to their belief in the promises of Jesus Christ. The Lord declared, "For whosoever will save his life shall lose it: and whosoever will lose his life for my sake shall find it" (Matthew 16:25).

Notes

1. F. J. Foakes Jackson, *The Rise of Gentile Christianity*.

2. Sir W.M. Ramsey, *The Bearing of Recent Discoveries on the Trustworthiness of the New Testament* (London: Hodder and Stoughton, 1915).

3. F. F. Bruce, "Archeological Confirmation of the New Testament," *Revelation and the Bible*, ed. Carl Henry (Grand Rapids: Baker House, 1969).

4. Samuel H. Moffett, *A History of Christianity in Asia* (Mary Knoll: Orbis Books, 1998).

5. Cicero, *Vin Verrem* 64, 66.

6. Sebastien Tillemont, *Memoires* (1712) 324.

7. Eusebius, *The Epistle of the Church of Smyrna, Nicene and Post Nicene Fathers* (Edinburgh: T. & T. Clark, 1991).

8. Truman C. Davis, "The Crucifixion of Jesus," *Arizona Medicine* March 1965.

9. David Frederick Strauss, *The Life of Jesus for the People*, 2nd ed. (London: Williams and Norgate, 1879) 1: 412.

10. Phlegon, *Olympiads*.

11. Philopon, *De. Opif. Mund. II* 21.

12. Julius Africanus, *Extant Writings* 18, *Ante-Nicene Fathers*, 10 vols. (Edinburgh: T. & T. Clark, 1991) vol. 6.

13. Arthur M. Ramsey, *God, Christ and the World* (London: SCM Press, 1969) 78–80.

14. Flavius Josephus, *Antiquities of the Jews* (Grand Rapids: Kregel Publications, 1974) vol. 18.

15. R. C. Stone, ZPEG, vol. 3: 697.

16. A. T. Robertson, *Word Pictures in the New Testament* (New York: R. R. Smith, Inc., 1931) 239.

17. Paul H. Hoch, Joseph Zubin and Grhune Stratton, eds., *Psychopathology of Perception* (New York, 1965).

18. Thomas James Thorburn, *The Resurrection Narratives and Modern Criticism* (London: Kegan Paul, Trench, Trubner & Co., Ltd., 1910).

8

The Intermediate State After Death

Do the Dead Sleep Until the Final Resurrection?

A popular but erroneous notion is that Christians who die in the faith somehow rest unconsciously through centuries of soul sleep until the final Day of Judgment when they will be resurrected to joyful consciousness in their heavenly home. The prophet Daniel spoke of the final resurrection of both the wicked and the righteous souls at the last day: "And many of them that sleep in the dust of the earth shall awake, some to everlasting life, and some to shame and everlasting contempt" (Daniel 12:2). However, despite Daniel's expression "them that sleep in the dust of the earth," the Bible teaches that our souls remain conscious forever. Therefore, it is our bodies that are described as being "asleep."

While our dead bodies are said to "rest" or "sleep," the Scriptures always refer to the departed soul as being conscious. A powerful confirmation of this important doctrine is found in Christ's own words to the repentant thief on the cross. Christ promised, "Verily I say unto thee, today shalt thou be with me in paradise" (Luke 23:43). This statement confirms that the spirit of the repentant thief immediately awakened from death that very day. The souls of Christians who die will immediately awaken to a joyful reunion with Jesus Christ and the departed saints in the New Jerusalem. Therefore, the common concept of soul sleep, the suggestion that the soul sleeps in the grave, is wrong. This false doctrine arose from the mistake of identifying our spirit, which immediately goes to Heaven, with our physical body, which *does* rest or sleep in the dust of the earth until the moment of our final resurrection.

The truth about the soul's consciousness in Heaven after our death is also confirmed in the teaching of the apostle Paul: "We are confident, I say, and willing rather to be absent from the body, and to be present with the Lord" (2 Corinthians 5:8). In other words, Paul affirms that the moment a Christian's soul leaves his body, his spirit will be consciously aware and in the presence of Jesus in Heaven.

Do Christians Go to an Intermediate Place Before Heaven?

Countless Christians over the centuries have been deceived by a false teaching to believe that they must be punished temporarily for their sins before they are finally permitted to enter the gates of Heaven. This false concept of a "purgatory" is contradicted by the teaching of Jesus to the repentant thief on the cross and the teaching of the apostle Paul (2 Corinthians 5:8). Over the centuries, many in the medieval Church in Rome were taught and believed that there is a spiritual place called purgatory where the souls of Christians must endure a degree of punishment equivalent to their sins prior to their ultimate entrance into Heaven. However, this view has no biblical base. The concept of purgatory has no foundation in the Bible whatsoever. Furthermore, the concept rejects the Atonement, Christ's completed justification to forgive our sins and pay the whole price of our personal salvation and achieve our reconciliation to God.

In his book, *Man All Immortal*,[1] Bishop Clark wrote about the doctrine of purgatory. "It is really astonishing when we consider how widely this spurious doctrine of a separate abode has spread, and how long it has prevailed in the Christian Church, despite the fact that it has no authority from the Bible. This false doctrine of purgatory is derived from an incorrect understanding of the biblical word *hades*."

The concept of purgatory developed gradually over the centuries, as many people looked to tradition rather than base their beliefs directly on the inspired Word of God. Although there are no biblical passages that support it, there is one curious passage in a nonbiblical, apocryphal manuscript written in the centuries before Christ lived. This document is often quoted at the source of this concept.

Known as 2 *Maccabees*, this manuscript is a historical account of the Jewish wars to win political and religious independence from the pagan Greeks, who ruled Syria and Israel in 169 to 162 B.C. While this book is historically interesting, it is not inspired. Therefore, it should not be used to establish a doctrine for Christianity.

The passage in this manuscript that leads some scholars to support the notion of purgatory is this: After burying some Jewish soldier who had sinfully worshipped pagan idols, the Israelite general Judas Maccabee led prayers for the dead men. The soldiers "betook themselves unto prayer, and besought Him that the sin committed might wholly be put out of remembrance." Later he "sent to Jerusalem to offer a sin offering . . . in that he was mindful of the resurrection: for if he had not hoped that they that were slain should have risen again, it had been superfluous and vain to pray for the dead. . . . Whereupon he made a reconciliation for the dead, that they might be delivered from sin" (2 *Maccabees* 12:42–45).

Between Death and the Resurrection: What Happens to Our Soul?

Great confusion exists in the minds of many people about the temporary destiny, condition, and location of the souls of both believers and nonbelievers from the moment of their death until they reach their soul's final destination of Heaven or Hell. The Bible reveals that the spiritual experience of sinners and saints after their death is quite different, even before the final judgment before God. The Old Testament speaks of "hades" as the immediate but temporary destination of departed souls and the "grave" as the location of the dead bodies.

Recently, some scholars have suggested that the doctrine of bodily and spiritual resurrection was not known to the Hebrews of the Old Testament. This is simply untrue. From the first book of the Bible, Genesis, until the last book, Malachi, we find numerous inspired statements proving that the writers of the Old Testament Scriptures clearly taught the reality of a bodily resurrection and a final judgment before God in Heaven based on the individual's personal actions and beliefs. In Genesis we repeatedly find the statement that the patriarchs were "gathered to their Fathers," even in the case of Jacob, whose body was not actually buried with his ancestors for many years. This statement proves that Moses and the patriarchs knew that their souls would be reunited with the souls of God's people who had died before them.

Job, possibly the oldest book in the Bible, reveals his personal anticipation of a physical resurrection of his body and its union with his soul in the last days. "For I know that my redeemer liveth, and that he shall stand at the latter day upon the earth: And though after my skin worms destroy this body, yet in my flesh shall I see God"(Job 19:25–26). Later, the prophet Daniel described the final two resurrections of humanity — one into spiritual life and the other into spiritual death: "Many of them that sleep in the dust of the earth shall awake, some to everlasting life, and some to shame and everlasting contempt" (Daniel 12:2).

The prophet John wrote the book of Revelation almost six centuries after Daniel. In it, he revealed additional inspired truth about the resurrection. The first resurrection will include those saints who accepted salvation. It will be completed at the beginning of the one thousand year millennium. Meanwhile, the second resurrection will include those who rejected salvation, choosing instead to be judged at the Great White Throne Judgement at the end of the thousand year millennium. All those who partake in any of the many stages of the first resurrection will be saved. All those who die rejecting God's mercy will participate in the second resurrection, ending in complete spiritual death and Hell.

Hades, the Place of Waiting for the Unsaved Souls

Many people speak and teach as though wicked sinners who reject Christ's salvation go immediately to Hell after they die. However, the Bible clearly states that the souls of unrepentant sinners descend after death into a place called *hades*, specifically, that part of hades called the place of torment, to await the final Great White Throne Judgment that will occur at the end of the Millennium. Christ described the state of the wicked dead when He spoke of the sinful rich man who went to hades. "And it came to pass, that the beggar died, and was carried by the angels into Abraham's bosom: the rich man also died, and was buried; And in Hell [*hades*] he lift up his eyes, being in torments, and seeth Abraham afar off, and Lazarus in his bosom. And he cried and said, Father Abraham, have mercy on me, and send Lazarus, that he may dip the tip of his finger in water, and cool my tongue; for I am tormented in this flame" (Luke 16:22–24). From this passage and others, the Bible reveals that sinners descend into hades and remain there in torment until the final Great White Throne Judgment, which will send them to an eternity without Christ in Hell. In fact, according to the Scriptures, neither Satan nor his demons, nor unrepentant sinners, will go to Hell until God's final judgment after the Millennium, at the Great White Throne in Heaven. Judgment Day for all of the souls who reject God's salvation will occur in Heaven after Jesus defeats Satan at the end of the thousand year Millennium.

Abraham's Bosom

The words of Christ reveal that all of the souls of those who died as believers in God before Christ's resurrection went to a place of waiting and comfort in hades known as Abraham's Bosom. Although Jesus' words reveal that the souls of people in both areas of hades were aware of each other, it was impossible for anyone to cross over from one place to the other. Abraham declared, "And beside all this, between us and you there is a great gulf fixed: so that they which would pass from hence to you cannot; neither can they pass to us, that would come from thence" (Luke 16:26). All of the Old Testament believers in God were taken to Abraham's Bosom to await their ultimate passage into Heaven. However, the Gospel of Matthew states that after Christ arose from the empty tomb, many graves were opened: "And many bodies of the saints which slept arose, And came out of the graves after his resurrection, and went into the holy city, and appeared unto many" (Matthew 27:52,53). This tremendous miracle of resurrecting the bodies and souls of many of the Old Testament saints demonstrated that Christ defeated the power of sin and death forever for all who placed their faith in Him.

Just as He resurrected those Old Testament saints, someday Jesus Christ will resurrect the bodies of all living and departed Christian believers, at the Rapture of the Church. Those "many" who arose and went into the Holy City proved the power of Christ's resurrection to the people of Jerusalem. Despite overwhelming opposition, the truth of the resurrection of Christ and of these "firstfruits" saints spread like wildfire throughout the Roman empire until, by the end of the second century, a huge portion of the population followed Christ.

Paradise: The New Jerusalem, the City of the Redeemed

A major transformation occurred in the spiritual condition of the departed Old Testament spirits when Jesus Christ defeated Satan through His death and supernatural resurrection when "He led captivity captive" (Ephesians 4:8). "The captivity of death" was defeated when Jesus triumphed over Satan and led many of the departed saints in Abraham's Bosom home to Heaven. While the Scriptures do not state specifically that these resurrected saints immediately ascended to Heaven when Jesus ascended, the commonly held teaching of the early Church asserted this. Certainly, they would not have physically died again. In all probability they ascended into Heaven at the very moment Jesus Christ ascended — forty days after His resurrection — "in a cloud of witnesses." From the time of Christ's death on the cross, the souls of believers who died went immediately to a place called Paradise. Jesus declared to the thief on the cross, "Verily I say unto thee, To day shalt thou be with me in paradise" (Luke 23:43). Since the time of Jesus' resurrection, instead of descending into Abraham's Bosom when they died, all deceased believers now ascend immediately into Heaven to enjoy the presence of Jesus Christ forever.

Paradise is another biblical word used to describe the New Jerusalem, the city of God in Heaven that Christ is preparing for His Bride, the Church. In Paradise the souls of believers will enjoy forever the presence of Christ and the other saints throughout history who have died as believers. However, these souls do not yet possess their eternal resurrection bodies. These souls in Paradise eagerly await the day of Resurrection when they receive their new immortal, incorruptible bodies so that they might participate in all the experiences of Heaven and join with

Christ to rule the nations on earth. Paul wrote the following about this subject:

> For the earnest expectation of the creature waiteth for the manifestation of the sons of God. For the creature was made subject to vanity, not willingly, but by reason of him who hath subjected the same in hope, Because the creature itself also shall be delivered from the bondage of corruption into the glorious liberty of the children of God. For we know that the whole creation groaneth and travaileth in pain together until now. And not only they, but ourselves also, which have the firstfruits of the Spirit, even we ourselves groan within ourselves, waiting for the adoption, to wit, the redemption of our body (Romans 8:19–23).

The term "third Heaven" also refers to Paradise and the New Jerusalem. The three terms are identical, as Paul explains:

> It is not expedient for me doubtless to glory. I will come to visions and revelations of the Lord. I knew a man in Christ above fourteen years ago, (whether in the body, I cannot tell; or whether out of the body, I cannot tell: God knoweth;) such an one caught up to the third Heaven. And I knew such a man, (whether in the body, or out of the body, I cannot tell: God knoweth;) How that he was caught up into paradise, and heard unspeakable words, which it is not lawful for a man to utter (2 Corinthians 121–4).

Later, in Revelation 2:7 John confirms that Paradise is identical to the New Jerusalem. The prophet records Jesus Christ's promise about His Heavenly city, the New

Jerusalem: "To him that overcometh will I give to eat of the tree of life, which is in the midst of the paradise of God" (Revelation 2:7).

Souls Who Died Without Repenting

In His parable about the rich man and the beggar, Jesus taught that the rich man who died unrepentant was totally conscious, not only of his torment, but also of the existence of his brothers on earth who were living carelessly and in danger of suffering his same fate. The Bible taught that all of the Old Testament's righteous souls went to a place of spiritual rest in hades called Abraham's Bosom. There these souls pleasantly awaited the time when Christ's resurrection would release them to enter Heaven. Peter refers to this resurrection event: "By which also he went and preached unto the spirits in prison" (1 Peter 3:19). Matthew's gospel teaches that many of those righteous saints were physically resurrected at the same time that Jesus rose from the grave (Matt. 27:52–53).

However, after the Resurrection hades became the waiting place for only the unrepentant souls who rejected God's salvation before and after the resurrection of Jesus. The spirits of these unrepentant sinners abide consciously in hades until the time of their ultimate judgment. The Scriptures reveal that the souls of the unsaved are not sent to Hell itself after death (Matthew 25:41, 2 Thessalonians 1:7–10, Revelation 14:10–11; 20:10–15). Those who die without faith will exist in a spiritual state of torment, as a result of their unrepentant sins, until they finally appear before the Great White Throne in Heaven, following the Millennium.

The Gospel writer Luke records Christ's teaching about the state of the lost in hades.

> And it came to pass, that the beggar died, and was carried by the angels into Abraham's bosom: the rich man also died, and was buried; And in Hell he lift up his eyes, being in torments, and seeth Abraham afar off, and Lazarus in his bosom. And he cried and said, Father Abraham, have mercy on me, and send Lazarus, that he may dip the tip of his finger in water, and cool my tongue; for I am tormented in this flame. But Abraham said, Son, remember that thou in thy lifetime receivedst thy good things, and likewise Lazarus evil things: but now he is comforted, and thou art tormented. And beside all this, between us and you there is a great gulf fixed: so that they which would pass from hence to you cannot; neither can they pass to us, that would come from thence. Then he said, I pray thee therefore, father, that thou wouldst send him to my father's house: For I have five brethren; that he may testify unto them, lest they also come into this place of torment (Luke 16:22–28).

One of the great horrors of hades for those who reject God's mercy in this life is that they are capable of sensing that those who accepted God's salvation are separated from them by an impassable barrier, "a great gulf." Jesus described the despair of the unrighteous rich man who saw that the beggar had been accepted by God: "And beside all this, between us and you there is a great gulf fixed: so that they which would pass from hence to you cannot; neither can they pass to us, that would come from thence" (Luke 16:26).

Throughout our life on earth the offer of Christ's salvation is available to us each at every moment if we will only turn from our sinful life and repent of our sins to Him. However, the Scriptures repeatedly warn us that each of us will finally come to a point in our life when we are no longer able to accept Christ's offer of salvation — that moment is our death. Despite the final spiritual awareness that will be available to those who have died in their sins still rejecting Christ's offer of salvation, it will be too late for them.

The final judgment of unrepentant sinners will occur before Jesus Christ at the Great White Throne at the end of the Millennium. All of the unsaved will be physically resurrected at that time to receive their resurrection bodies for eternity. They will then be judged based on God's infallible records of their unconfessed sins and evil works. "And I saw a great white throne, and him that sat on it, from whose face the earth and the Heaven fled away; and there was found no place for them. And I saw the dead, small and great, stand before God; and the books were opened" (Rev. 20:11–12).

The Souls Who Repented Are Now in Paradise

The Bible teaches that the soul is neither annihilated at death, nor does it sleep. The body is described as sleeping in a sense because it rests in the earth until God resurrects it into a new immortal and spiritual body fit for eternity. The word cemetery is derived from the early Christians' proclamation that the body would eventually arise from sleep at the coming resurrection. However, the Bible never speaks of the soul as sleeping. The clear teaching of Scripture is that Christians immediately join Christ in Heaven at the moment of death. When the thief on the cross turned in faith to Jesus he said: "Lord, remember me when thou comest into thy kingdom. And Jesus said unto him, Verily I say unto thee, To day shalt thou be with me in paradise" (Luke

23:42–43). This paradise is identical with the New Jerusalem, the capital city of Heaven.

In the book of Revelation, John prophesied that those in Heaven, "rest not day and night, but actively serve God day and night in joyful worship." In the Old Testament, several passages speak of death as sleep and seem to describe *sheol* as a condition of unconsciousness. However, upon closer examination we find that each time the passage refers to the condition of the dead body, not the soul. One example that is sometimes quoted in favor of the concept of soul-sleep is the words of Solomon: "Whatsoever thy hand findeth to do, do it with thy might; for there is no work, nor device, nor knowledge, nor wisdom, in the grave, whither thou goest" (Ecclesiastes 9:10). In this passage Solomon is clearly referring to the condition of the inactivity of the body in the grave, not the soul. As confirmation of this interpretation, in the final chapter of Ecclesiastes, King Solomon affirms the destiny of the soul, as opposed to the body: "Then shall the dust return to the earth as it was: and the spirit shall return unto God who gave it" (Ecclesiastes 5:7).

The Hebrew word *sheol* appears sixty-five times in the Old Testament. It is translated thirty-one times as "Hell," and thirty-four times as "the grave" or "the pit." Each time the verse refers to the grave or the state of the body, never to the condition of the eternal soul. The New Testament uses the Greek word *hades* eleven times, and ten of those clearly refer to the place of the dead body, not the spirit.

If Jesus Christ does not return during our generation to resurrect His believers, then every living believer will someday experience Paradise in that intermediate state prior to the final resurrection day. When the resurrection occurs, all saints throughout history shall receive a glorious new resurrection bodies like that of Christ after He arose from death. Since Paradise is the next destination for those who love Christ, it is vital that we come to a full, biblically based understanding of the reality that awaits each of us on the other side of death.

The apostle Paul alluded to Paradise being a place more pleasant than Abraham's Bosom, the place that the Old Testament saints entered following their death. Speaking of the great patriarchs of the Hebrew race, Paul wrote, "And these all, having obtained a good report through faith, received not the promise: God having provided some better thing for us, that they without us should not be made perfect" (Hebrews 11:39–40). While death involves the immediate transfer of the spirit of a Christian believer to the New Jerusalem in Heaven, we will not receive our resurrection bodies until the time of Christ's return in the air to resurrect all of the saints, both the living believers and the millions of departed saints who are already in Paradise with Jesus. Paul spoke of the body as the clothing of the human spirit and indicated clearly that the spirits of the departed are unclothed or disembodied until the Rapture. The apostle wrote, "For we that are in this tabernacle do groan, being burdened: not for that we would be unclothed, but clothed upon, that mortality might be swallowed up of life" (2 Corinthians 5:4). The prophet Israel foresaw the final resurrection when all saints will finally be clothed with a resurrection body. "He will swallow up death in victory; and the Lord God will wipe away tears from off all faces" (Isaiah 25:8).

Do the Saints Become Angels?

One of the more popular but erroneous ideas that has confused people over the centuries is the mistaken idea that departed saints become angels after they die. However, the clear teaching of the Scriptures is that angels are a separate class of spiritual beings, distinct from humans, who were created in the beginning by Jesus Christ for a particular spiritual purpose. The Bible teaches that angels perform a ministry as God's messengers and that they watch over the saints as guardians. It is natural that some Christians who are biblically uninformed might form the erroneous impression that our departed loved ones may perform that guardian role out of their continued affection for their loved ones left behind. However, many passages of Scripture clearly distinguish the angels from the departed human saints. One scriptural example alone will prove that humans are distinct from angels. The apostle Paul wrote, "Know ye not that we shall judge angels? How much more things that pertain to this life? (1 Corinthians 6:3). The fact that the saints will ultimately judge the fallen angels demonstrates that we belong to a different class of created beings than angels.

What Happens When Babies Die?

> The gates of Heaven are so easily found when we are little, and they are always standing open to let children wander in.[2]

Is there anyone whose heart is not stirred at the premature passing away of a young child or baby? There is something that seems fundamentally unjust about the death of an innocent child who dies long before its expected time. Yet, in the mysterious providence of a merciful God, it may be that our heavenly Father has spared that child from some great tragedy or a life that would have ended in spiritual rebellion and terrible suffering. Only God knows the future of the path we tread. The ancient poet Menander wrote, "Whom the gods love dies young."[3]

The clear teaching of the Bible is that the souls of those children who die before they reach the age of understanding and responsibility are taken to the New Jerusalem with Christ to live joyfully with Him until the day of resurrection when they shall receive their own immortal body fit for eternity. We know that children who die immediately go to Heaven from several different passages of Scripture. When King David's son, born of Bathsheba, died after seven days, the king stopped weeping and declared, "But now he is dead, wherefore should I fast? can I bring him back again? I shall go to him, but he shall not return to me" (2 Samuel 12:23). David's inspired declaration that "I shall go to him" acknowledges the fact that his baby went directly to Heaven. David's inspired words assure us that we will recognize our loved ones when we are reunited with them in Heaven, even as David will be reunited with his beloved son.

The salvation of children who die in youth is confirmed also by the tender words of Jesus to His disciples, who tried to drive away the children who surrounded Him. "But when Jesus saw it, he was much displeased, and said unto them, Suffer the little children to come unto me, and forbid them not: for of such is the kingdom of God" (Mark 10:14).

Throughout history the vast majority of humans never survived long enough to reach maturity. The ravages of childhood diseases, epidemics, starvation, and ever-present violence of wars killed the vast majority of young children long before they reached spiritual maturity. Even today, in Third World countries, the mortality rate of children is appalling. It is comforting to know that these children have a birthright in the world to come. Jesus said, "Of such is the kingdom of Heaven" (Matthew 9:13–15).

There are several theories expressed by theologians regarding the destiny of the souls of young children who die before reaching spiritual maturity. The generally taught, though unofficial, position of the Roman Catholic Church is that children who die unbaptized will not enter Heaven, rather they will enter a spiritually neutral place known as "limbo."[4] Some Calvinist groups suggested that deceased children go to Hell because, possessing a human nature, they are sinners at birth, due to humanity's Fall. Other Calvinist groups, however, deny this doctrine. The most commonly taught doctrine by the majority of Protestant churches is that all young children who die will experience personal salvation and are immediately taken to Heaven to live with Jesus Christ.

Since the Bible teaches that all humans are born with a sinful nature and are thus deserving of spiritual death in Hell, the salvation of young children is due to the fact that Jesus Christ died on the cross for their sins. Jesus said, "Verily I say unto you, Except ye be converted, and become as little children, ye shall not enter into the kingdom of Heaven. Whosoever therefore shall humble himself as this little child, the same is greatest in the kingdom of Heaven" (Matthew 18:3–4).

Though temporarily parted from their parents and family, children who die are taken into the care of the Lord Himself while they await their future joyous family reunion with loved ones in Paradise. Death cannot defeat our love; it can only delay it. One additional reason for our assurance that young children who die go to Heaven is found in the passage in Revelation 20, which describes the Great White Throne Judgment of God. The prophet John wrote, "And I saw the dead, small and great, stand before God; and the books were opened: and another book was opened, which is the book of life: and the dead were judged out of those things which were written in the books, according to their works"

(Revelation 20:12). It is clear from this prophecy about the Great White Throne Judgment that the dead were judged by those things that were written in the books, according to their works. Obviously, a significant part of individual judgment for those who will go to Hell depends on their deeds and works. Since it is obvious that a young child who dies cannot have accomplished any works or committed any evil deeds upon which they can be fairly judged, they will go to Heaven.

At some point the atonement of Christ's blood must be applied to the heart of that child to enable him to receive a new spiritual life in Jesus so that he can partake of the joys of eternal life in Heaven. This is one of those areas where we must trust the love and justice of God until we see His unfolding purpose and plan in Heaven. The patriarch Abraham successfully pleaded with God to be merciful to his nephew and his family who were dwelling in the wicked city of Sodom. Abraham declared, "Shall not the Judge of all the earth do right?" (Genesis 18:25)

Just as a child matures and develops in his earthly life, those who die as children will develop into fully mature members of the family of God. There will be abundant opportunities for the fullest development of all the gifts that God has given us when we arrive in Heaven. These children will enjoy the tender love of Christ and of angels while receiving their celestial education. Furthermore, the New Testament passage that tells us that John the Baptist was filled with the Holy Spirit in his mother's womb provides compelling evidence that an unborn fetus does possess an eternal soul. The Heavenly city contains hundreds of millions of children who died before they were born. When you consider the billions who have died as infants and unborn babies over the thousands of years of man's existence, it is probable that this group of souls forms a majority of the human inhabitants in the New Jerusalem.

Notes

1. Bishop Clark, *Man All Immortal*: 189.
2. Sir James Matthew, *Sentimental Tommy* (New York: Charles Scribner's Sons).
3. Menander, *Dis Exapaton*.
4. Karl Rahner, ed., *Encyclopedia of Theology* (New York: The Seabury Press, 1975) 850–851.

9

God's Promise of Resurrection

> But some man will say, How are the dead raised up? And with what body do they come? (1 Corinthians 15:35)
>
> Behold, I show you a mystery; We shall not all sleep, but we shall all be changed, In a moment, in the twinkling of an eye, at the last trump: for the trumpet shall sound, And the dead shall be raised incorruptible, and we shall be changed. For this corruptible must put on incorruption, and this mortal must put on immortality. (1 Corinthians 15:51–53).

The Bible tells us plainly that once we participate in the resurrection, we will receive a spiritual, yet physical, body like the body Christ revealed to His disciples after His resurrection. This spiritual body will have the human appearance of our present "earthly" body. Although our earthly bodies are "corruptible," and therefore subject to sickness and decay, our new bodies will be "incorruptible," not subject to accident, disease, or decay. Our present mortal body will be transformed into an immortal spiritual body that will never die.

For thousands of years Christians have confidently expected that they will be reunited with their departed loved ones in Heaven. In Revelation, John saw "a great number that no man could number" surrounding the throne of God in Heaven. He immediately identified this multitude of individuals as resurrected saints, not angels. This passage confirms that saints in Heaven possess the distinct appearance of men, not of angels or disembodied spirits. The nature of humans, created in "the image of God," requires that we inhabit a personal and individual physical body with an immortal spirit that will transcend the finite limits of this short life on earth. The apostle Paul raised a profound question, "But some men will say, How are the dead raised up? and with what body do they come?" (1 Corinthians 15:35). Later in the passage Paul answers this key question by revealing the following truth:

> It is sown a natural body; it is raised a spiritual body. There is a natural body, and there is a spiritual body. And so it is written, The first man Adam was made a living soul; the last Adam was made a quickening spirit. Howbeit that was not first which is spiritual, but that which is natural; and afterward that which is spiritual. The first man is of the earth, earthy: the

> second man is the Lord from Heaven. (1 Corinthians 15:44–47)

The Lord contrasts the natural and spiritual bodies. The natural body is the normal human one that Adam and all humans possess here on earth. Our new spiritual body will be given to us by God at the Resurrection to prepare us for eternity in both Heaven and on earth.

Several centuries ago the great French religious philosopher, Blaise Pascal, wrote about the resurrection of our bodies. In criticism of the attacks of atheists on this foundational doctrine of Christianity, Pascal wrote:

> What reason have atheists for saying that we cannot rise again? Which is the more difficult, to be born, or to rise again? That what has never been, should be, or that, what has been, should be again? Is it more difficult to come into being than to return to it?[1]

God created every one of us by fusing the microscopic sperm and ova of our parents to produce the complete complex genetic code that is the blueprint for every one of the 50 trillion cells in our body. If God could create a human originally, it seems obtuse to reject the possibility that He couldn't recreate this same body in the future.

Our New Resurrection Body

The Bible tells us that we are individual human beings, now and forever. We shall stand in the Last Day as individuals to meet Jesus Christ as either our Judge or our Savior. Our new spiritual bodies will be transformed and made glorious by Christ in the Rapture. Each body will still retain the unique imprint given by our Creator. The same awesome, intelligent God who designed our natural body with such particular care has also designed a future heavenly body for us to live in forever. The book of Job teaches clearly that we will be resurrected in the last days in our own restored bodies. Job wrote, "And though after my skin worms destroy this body, yet in my flesh shall I see God" (Job 19:26).

Over three centuries ago the Puritan reformers at the Westminster Assembly created the *Westminster Confession of Faith* to reflect their understanding of Scripture regarding various important doctrines. After much debate, the Westminster Assembly declared that all of the dead "shall be raised up with the self-same bodies, and none other."[2] It is historically interesting to note that the Christian churches' opposition to cremation was originally based on the perception that burning the body would interfere with the future resurrection of the earthly body. However, the real reason Christians have typically avoided cremation is that both the Old and New Testaments teach that all of the saints were buried, symbolizing their hope of bodily resurrection in the last days. The practice of cremation originated in pagan cultures, where the expectation was that the soul would be reincarnated, not resurrected. Although cremation is obviously not the scriptural pattern for dealing with the body after death, God is certainly capable of resurrecting the body of anyone who has died, regardless of the nature of their death or method of internment.

Many agnostic critics suggest that the bodily resurrection of the saints is impossible if the physical body is destroyed. Some have questioned how a body could be physically resurrected after a person had been eaten by a shark, and had become part of the food chain. A famous example of this curious criticism of resurrection is found in the writings of the French atheistic philosopher Voltaire, who ridiculed the doctrine of resurrection. He proposed a hypothetical situation where a starving soldier was forced by circumstances to eat an Iroquois Indian he had killed, who himself had fed recently on some Jesuit priests. Voltaire contemptuously asked, "How is each to take again precisely what belongs to him? And what part belongs to each?"[3] The French philosopher Rousseau wrote a letter disputing this argument, saying, "All the subtleties of metaphysics will never make me doubt for a moment the immortality of the soul and a beneficent providence. . . . I feel it, I believe it, I want it, I hope for it. I will defend it to my last breath."

While this philosophical problem suggested by Voltaire and others seems to pose a problem for the biblical doctrine of physical resurrection, God is not subject to the finite limitations of our human mind. Many believers would answer this question by replying that God is quite as capable of resurrecting a body of a man as He is of creating his body the first time in his mother's womb. A possible answer to Voltaire's objection to physical resurrection is that every one of the 50 trillion cells in our bodies, even the smallest cell of our hair or skin, contains the complete DNA genetic code through which God programmed the complete body of every one of us from the moment of our conception. Every one of these cells contains the complete genetic information to reconstruct our complete body, down to our particular tastes in music or food.

Biologists have discovered that our physical body constantly renews itself at the cellular level. In fact, every seven years almost every one of these cells has been completely replaced by new cells. Therefore, in the natural course of a normal human life, our body will use and discard trillions of cells that are scattered throughout our homes, offices, etc. The enormous quantity of discarded cells would be enough to make up our body several times over. Since God would only need one single cell of our body with its complete DNA genetic code to recreate our body, there should be no real difficulty in God locating one single cell, regardless of what happens to the body after death.

Some have wondered if our resurrection body will appear to be the same age as our body when we died. While the Scriptures do not address this issue directly, the fourth-century theologian, St. Augustine of Hippo, suggested that every resurrected body would appear to be approximately thirty years old, the same age as Jesus Christ when He died. While this is a possible solution, we may have some choice in the matter. For example, the Gospels record that both Moses and Elijah appeared to the disciples of Christ on the Mount of Transfiguration. Since Moses was approximately 120 years old at his death, and Elijah was approximately 50 when he was taken, the Gospel's description may imply that these two saints appeared as their apparent age at death when they left this world. If Moses had appeared to the disciples as a young man they would probably not have recognized him as the great prophet of Israel. We will not know the answer to this question until we arrive in Heaven ourselves.

A Body Fit for Eternity

> For our citizenship is in Heaven, from which we also eagerly wait for the Savior, the Lord Jesus Christ, who will transform our lowly body that it may be conformed to . . . the working by which He is able even to subdue all things to Himself. (Philippians 3:20–21)

The clearest indication that we have of the nature of our

future spiritual body was shown to us in the resurrection of Jesus Christ. He appeared to His disciples and His followers on many occasions during the forty days after He rose from the grave. The Scriptures specifically promised us that our own resurrected bodies would be like His (Philippians 3:20–21; 1 John 3:2). Jesus knew the tendency of humans to assume that life after death would be some ghost-like and non-material existence. Jesus taught us clearly that our body will be real when we are resurrected:

> Jesus himself stood in the midst of them, And saith unto them, Peace be unto you. But they were terrified and affrighted, and supposed that they had seen a spirit. And he said unto them, Why are ye troubled? and why do thoughts arise in your hearts? Behold my hands and my feet, that it is I myself: handle me, and see; for a spirit hath not flesh and bones, as ye see me have. And when he had thus spoken, he showed them his hands and his feet. And while they yet believed not for joy, and wondered, he said unto them, Have ye here any meat? And they gave him a piece of a broiled fish, and of an honeycomb. And he took it, and did eat before them. (Luke 24:36–43)

On Sunday, the first day of the week, when Jesus rose from the dead He appeared to His disciples physically. His resurrected body was tangible; they could actually touch it. Later, He invited the doubter, Thomas, to put his finger on the scars in His wrists, and his hand on the scar on His side. His wrists and feet were still scarred from His wounds on the cross. Jesus showed that both His body and our resurrection bodies will have "flesh and bones" (Luke 24:39). Some have concluded erroneously from this verse that Luke taught that Jesus did not have any blood in His resurrected body. However, the verse simply describes His physical resurrection body as including "flesh and bones"; it does not state He had no blood. Jesus ate fish and drank with His disciples, demonstrating that He still experienced and enjoyed sensations, including taste.

The book of Revelation teaches that every one of God's resurrected saints will participate in the glorious "marriage supper of the Lamb" in Heaven following the Rapture. We will eat and drink with our Lord Jesus Christ and all of the other saints at the Marriage Supper, and forever afterward. The glorious "marriage supper of the lamb" will celebrate the final spiritual union of the Bride of Christ, the Christian saints, with the Bridegroom, Jesus Christ. In contemplation of this moment the British mystical poet Henry Vaughan wrote in 1660, "Look down, Great Master of the feast; O shine, And turn once more our water into wine!"

Although Jesus' body was like His body's appearance prior to His death, there was an indefinable and ethereal quality about Christ's resurrected appearance that caused Mary and His disciples to initially fail to recognize Him when they first met. Mary did not know Jesus when He first appeared to her outside the empty tomb. Neither did the two disciples walking on the road to Emmaus. This could be partly explained by the fact that they had not really expected that He would truly rise from the dead. And yet recognition did come eventually. Ultimately, hundreds of individuals recognized Jesus, including many of the disciples and His personal friends.

Meeting Loved Ones in Heaven

Although our bodies will be transformed at the Resurrection into an immortal and incorruptible form, we will still retain our human characteristics and physical appearance that will make us recognizable to those who have known us on earth. We will also be recognized by that great "cloud of witnesses," including those saints who never knew us on earth. The Scriptures declare, "Wherefore seeing we also are compassed about with so great a cloud of witnesses, let us lay aside every weight, and the sin which doth so easily beset us, and let us run with patience the race that is set before us" (Hebrews 12:1). The disciples recognized Elijah and Moses on the Mount of Transfiguration even though they had never met them before. Jesus said that the rich man recognized Abraham and the beggar while he was in Hades. It appears that our recognizable personalities and unique physical appearance will transcend the finite limits of this earthly existence, as we enter into our glorious heavenly inheritance.

Some have hypothesized that there we may have some choice regarding the matter of our future appearance. Possibly, those who die later in life may choose to have their resurrection body display the appearance of a young adult. A child who dies at the age of three may choose a mature body in Heaven. Some may choose to have the same physical appearance as when they died. Whatever the outward physical expression, our intellectual and spiritual nature in Heaven will be that of a mature saint having complete mental and physical faculties so that we may enjoy all that Christ has prepared for us. Our aged parents, who may have lost some of their physical vigor in their later years, will meet us in Heaven with a rejuvenated and spiritual body, now able to enjoy everything that can be experienced there.

The glorious promise of the Scriptures is that all living believers will rise at the Rapture to meet Jesus Christ in the air. Our joy will be multiplied beyond measure when we arrive in Heaven to participate in the greatest family reunion in history. All the tears we have shed for departed believers will be wiped away in one moment of indescribable love and joy when we meet our loved ones again. Imagine the joy we will feel when we meet Abraham, David, Esther, Peter, and other believers who have gone to Heaven before us. But our greatest joy will come when we finally see Jesus face to face and fall down at His feet in worship and gratitude to Him for our precious salvation.

Emotions in the Afterlife

For the first time in our life we will no longer be subject to physical death, disease or decay, nor will we ever again suffer pain. We will possess "perfect" bodies that will be incorruptible and immortal. Jesus chose to display His scars from the crucifixion to prove to His followers that He had truly risen from the dead. It is possible that martyrs may choose to still bear the visible evidence of their suffering as a badge of honor. Jesus will resurrect the bodies of those saints who have been burned to ashes, devoured by wild animals, and the billions whose bodies were turned to dust in the grave. He will restore everything that was lost. If we lost limbs, sight, or hearing, or intellect because of disease or accident during our earthly lives, the Lord will recreate our new resurrected bodies in total perfection in Heaven. If we were married on earth, there is no reason to assume this special spiritual love relationship will end when we arrive in Heaven. God gave Adam and Eve the gift of marriage before they sinned against His commands. In the Song of Songs, King Solomon described his married love for his bride, the Queen of Sheba. This love poem symbolizes the wonderful love God has for His chosen Bride, the Church.

In fact, the Lord uses the sacred image of marriage

as a symbol of the eternal relationship of Jesus Christ to both Israel and His Church. The Scriptures do not indicate that Christians will have additional children in Heaven; therefore, many theologians have concluded that resurrected Christians will not experience physical married love relationships. The Church, the Bride of Christ, will be complete in its final number when the Rapture occurs. Since none of the saints will ever again die after the Resurrection, there will be no need for reproduction in Heaven. However, the spiritual essence of a pure, holy love must find its highest expression in an eternal cherishing of our loved ones. "For now we see through a glass, darkly; but then face to face: now I know in part; but then shall I know even as also I am known. And now abideth faith, hope, charity, these three; but the greatest of these is charity" (1 Corinthians 13:12–13). In Heaven we shall experience far greater joy, knowledge, and wonderful relationships than we have ever known on earth.

The University of the New Jerusalem

Some Christians express the fear that in Heaven they will not be able to enjoy all of the activities they enjoy on earth. They are afraid they will lose their knowledge and awareness of earthly relationships and human interests. But why should we? Heaven is a place we will enjoy immensely. Our creative talents will flourish there, and forever we will be able to acquire knowledge about the universe. We will be able to satisfy our unlimited curiosity about creation, history, and science. We will finally understand why certain events occurred as they did in history and in our personal lives. Just as we can see far more from a mountain peak than we can from a valley, in Heaven we will have far greater vision and awareness than we have on earth. Some psychologists estimate that even a great genius like Albert Einstein only utilized ten percent of his mental potential. When we receive our resurrection body we will finally be able to actualize the complete potential that God created in every one of us to accomplish far beyond our present dreams. Not only will our interests continue, they will be intensified when we can see the interrelated events in the world and witness how the sovereign hand of God continually moves in the lives of individuals and nations. From the vantage point of eternity we will understand the reality of Christ's words when He said, "For we wrestle not against flesh and blood, but against principalities, against powers, against the rulers of the darkness of this world, against spiritual wickedness in high places" (Ephesians 6:12).

If we are among "those who have fallen asleep" and our spirits go to be with Jesus in Heaven before the Resurrection, our spirits will be aware of these things long before we receive our resurrected bodies. The saints of the Church who are now in Paradise are already witnessing what happens here on earth. They are looking at events from the perspective of eternity; they are not limited only to what we can see here and now. The book of Hebrews declares that "we also are compassed about with so great a cloud of witnesses" (Hebrews 12:1). One of the reasons there are no tears, worry, or pain in Heaven is that the saints can finally observe life from the detached standpoint of eternity, understanding God's sovereign will and purpose in human events. While these saints may be aware of events on earth involving their loved ones, it is likely that they will not be troubled by these things; they are seeing everything from the vantage point of Heaven. John declares in Revelation that there will be no more sorrow, crying, or pain, "for the former things are passed away"(Revelation 21:4).

Our Immortal Personalities

Each day of our life we are building personal character and the essence of the mature person we shall be throughout eternity. With every decision we make, and every commitment and relationship we form, we are building the spiritual personality we will live with forever. While our characters can easily be influenced when we are young, by the age of thirty or forty, our characters are usually set for life — except for the possibility of a radical transformation that can happen when we are spiritually reborn through an encounter with Jesus Christ. Personal salvation through Christ frees us from our captivity to sin and evil to become truly free to follow Jesus into a new life filled with joy, peace, and a profound, overwhelming love of God and His children.

Throughout his ministry, the prophet Elijah fought vigorously against evil and idolatry. The prophet Malachi identified Elijah as one who will reappear as a witness in the last days (Malachi 4:5). In the book of Revelation the prophet John foretold the reappearance of these two prophets who will stand in the last days against the Antichrist during the Tribulation. The book of Revelation reveals that the resurrected prophet Elijah will manifest the same character and supernatural powers he displayed in ancient times when he fought against the wicked King Ahab and the pagan prophets of Baal.

In our Christian life, our daily devotions, prayers, worship, deeds, and fellowship with other Christians prepare us for our eternal destiny as citizens of the heavenly city of God. The Lord commands us to cultivate a spiritual and Christ-like personality:

Put on therefore, as the elect of God, holy and

> beloved, bowels of mercies, kindness, humbleness of mind, meekness, long suffering; Forbearing one another, and forgiving one another, if any man have a quarrel against any: even as Christ forgave you, so also do ye. And above all these things put on charity, which is the bond of perfectness. And let the peace of God rule in your hearts, to the which also ye are called in one body; and be ye thankful. Let the word of Christ dwell in you richly in all wisdom; teaching and admonishing one another in psalms and hymns and spiritual songs, singing with grace in your hearts to the Lord. And whatsoever ye do in word or deed, do all in the name of the Lord Jesus, giving thanks to God and the Father by him. (Colossians 3:12–17)

Christ agreed to die on the cross in order to save men from the horrors of an eternity in Hell. In the most incredible display of love ever known, Jesus Christ paid the complete price of the punishment of death and Hell for all of us. Paul declared:

> But God commendeth his love toward us, in that, while we were yet sinners, Christ died for us. Much more then, being now justified by his blood, we shall be saved from wrath through him. For if, when we were enemies, we were reconciled to God by the death of his Son, much more, being reconciled, we shall be saved by his life. For if when we were enemies we were reconciled to God through the death of His Son, much more, having been reconciled, we shall be saved by His life. (Romans 5:8–10)

The Resurrection of Jesus Christ

The historical truth about the physical resurrection of Jesus Christ from the grave is the essential bedrock upon which the entire Christian faith stands. The apostle Paul declared, "If Christ be not risen, then is our preaching vain, and your faith is also vain" (1 Corinthians 15:14). As I demonstrated in an earlier chapter, there is an enormous amount of historically verifiable evidence that Jesus Christ lived, died, and rose from the dead. Some people, having rejected Christ's claims, seek false comfort in believing that they will never have to face God as their judge at the end of their lives. They hope that when they die, all consciousness ceases. Therefore, they presume, why not "eat, drink and be merry for tomorrow we die?" This worldly epicurean philosophy totally opposes what the Bible teaches. The Scriptures teach that there is eternal life for every soul after death. Our bodies will undergo an instantaneous transformation and a supernatural transition at our resurrection to prepare us for eternity. Our natural bodies will die, but our soul and spirit live on forever in our new resurrection body.

One beautiful summer evening, the famous German philosopher and poet Goethe was walking on the road toward the city of Weimar at sunset with his friend and fellow author Johann Peter Eckermann. As they stood gazing at the majestic setting sun, Goethe exclaimed, "Setting, nevertheless the sun is always the same sun. I am fully convinced that our spirit is a being of a nature quite indestructible, and its activity continues from eternity to eternity." Goethe indicated his realization that, though to our natural eyes the soul of a man may die, it will forever retain its identity and consciousness.

The Early Churches' Hope of Immortality

During the centuries following the death of Christ, the early Christians often faced death and martyrdom with joy and hope in Christ, to the amazement of the pagan Romans. The Christians declared that they considered the grave as a mere resting place for their bodies until they would be resurrected and transformed by Christ at His second coming. They believed their departed spirits would be freed to rejoice in the living presence of God, enjoying a glorious and exciting life in Heaven. Early Christian texts remind us of their courage in the face of torture and imminent death. Their transforming belief in the resurrection of Christ, and the promise of Heaven, motivated these saints to bravely face their deaths with hymns of praise upon their lips. Between the second and fourth centuries, Christians often met secretly in subterranean catacombs deep beneath the city of Rome and other cities throughout the empire in order to worship, to hide, and to safely bury their dead. Inscriptions on these ancient tombs and catacombs in these tunnels reveal the early beliefs of the persecuted Christians buried there. These epitaphs convey that the early Church clearly taught the consciousness of the spirit after death, and that one day, in the future Rapture, our bodies would be resurrected by Christ.

One epitaph found in the catacombs beneath Rome contains this inscription: "Eutuchius, wise, pious and kind, believing in Christ, entered the portals of death, and has the reward of the light of Heaven." Another touching epitaph on the grave of a child contains the loving but hopeful message of immortality: "Here sleeps in the sleep of peace the sweet and innocent Severianus, whose spirit is received into the light of God." One coffin holding the body of a young woman named Prudentius revealed the following hopeful inscription that demonstrated the family's hope of the coming resurrection: "*Non nurtuased data somno* — She is not dead but sleepeth."

The universal belief of the early Christians in resurrection is demonstrated in these ancient inscriptions: "He sleeps but lives"; "He reposes in the Lord Jesus"; "The soul lives, unknowing of death, and consciously rejoices in the vision of Christ." One of the strongest statements is the following: "I believe, because my Redeemer lives, and in the last day shall raise me from the earth that in my flesh I shall see the Lord." This inscription reminds us of the statement of Job, "For I know that my redeemer liveth, and that he shall stand at the latter day upon the earth. And though after my skin worms shall destroy this body, yet in my flesh shall I see God" (Job 19:25–26).

The very idea of death as our final destiny was rejected by the early followers of Christ. Death to them was a mere transformation, a rebirth into our new eternal life with Christ in Heaven. In *Homily in Matthew*, John Chrysotom, a famous Christian writer from the fourth century, speaks of the hope of Christians who have died: "They say not of the departed, 'He is dead,' but he is perfected."

American preacher Reverend Henry Ward Beecher (1813–1887) wrote about his confidence as he contemplated his approaching death:

> I avow again, as I have before, may God give me a sudden death: I would rather have it instantaneous as lightning . . . but I would rather die with the harness on, in the midst of the battle. But as to the time, manner and place, that's God's will, not mine. Dying to me is not humiliation, but exaltation-

> emerging from that which is nothing but an egg, into the plenitude of power, into hope, into waves of affection and soul-loving that shall satisfy the amplitude of yearning in that direction. . . . I shall not die downward toward Hell, but upward toward Heaven. So let us shake the tree of life that the leaves of it will drop down for the healing of the nations.[4]

The remarkable honesty of the Gospel writers is evident in their writings. In each book, the author reveals his doubts, uncertainties, and failures of faith when their leader, Jesus of Nazareth, faced crucifixion. This unprecedented honesty provides powerful evidence that their historical accounts about the life, teachings, death, and resurrection of Christ are truthful. The natural tendency of human writers is to present the facts of a historical event in a manner that complements their intelligent foresight, wisdom, courage, and character. However, throughout the Gospels, from Matthew to John, we read about the human failings of the divinely inspired authors. These historical records are precisely what they claim to be — the divinely inspired writings of four disciples of Jesus who were commanded by God's Holy Spirit to record the events and teachings of Jesus of Nazareth.

The resurrection of Jesus forever transformed the concept of death from the dark fears of ancient paganism and the dim hopes of Judaism's promise of being "gathered to their fathers" into the triumphant Christian vision of an eternity in glory with God and the saints. Throughout ancient history, pagans mourned without true hope for their dead loved ones because their religions provided no firm information nor certain hope for a future life.

The Promise of Resurrection

Every human who lives and dies will rise ultimately rise again after death. However, there is a great difference between the destiny of those who accept Christ's forgiveness and those who reject His offer of salvation. The Bible describes two different resurrections: the first resurrection leads to spiritual life in Heaven and the second resurrection leads to spiritual death in Hell. The first resurrection will include every person throughout history who has repented of their sin and accepted the pardon of Christ. These souls will participate in the resurrection to eternal spiritual life. This first resurrection has several stages that includes different groups of saints who will be resurrected at different times. The Bible describes the initial group as the "firstfruits" who arose two thousand years ago with Jesus (Matthew 27:52–53). Then the Bible describes the future Rapture of all other Christian believers. Following the Rapture, a group of Jewish and Gentile "tribulation saints" who accept Christ as their Savior during the seven-year Tribulation period will also be resurrected when Christ returns at Armageddon, according to Matthew 24:40, when "one will be taken and the other left." All of the souls who participate in the various stages of this first resurrection to life will enjoy life in Heaven forever.

The second resurrection will include those who rejected God's pardon and chose to die in their sins. All of the unrepentant souls from Cain to the last rebel who dies in the final battle at the end of the Millennium will be resurrected in the Last Day to stand before the Great White Throne Judgment of God. Revelation 20:14 says, "This is the second death." Tragically all those who reject Christ's offer of salvation will participate in this second resurrection and experience spiritual death forever.

The First Resurrection to Eternal Life

The Bible uses the word "firstfruits" to describe the first resurrection, eternal life in Heaven. In Israel the Feast of Firstfruits occurred in the spring of the year to celebrate the first fruits of the harvest. The Jews brought these tokens of the bounty of the coming harvest to the Temple to acknowledge that God was the provider of the harvest. This word "firstfruits" became the symbol of this first group of resurrected saints, a token of the final great harvest when Jesus, the Lord of the Harvest, will descend in the air to gather the saints to meet Him, and return to Heaven.

The writer of the book of Hebrews, after recounting the many acts of faith of Old Testament saints, told his readers about their future life in Heaven. He declares, "We are surrounded by so great a cloud of witnesses" (Hebrews 12:1). They are still alive! They have been transformed and are now in Paradise, interested and observing our walk of faith. Many of those Old Testament saints participated in this first stage of the first resurrection, when they arose at the same moment when Jesus rose from the grave.

Matthew 27:52,53 describes the extraordinary events that occurred when Jesus rose from the dead, during the Feast of the Firstfruits: "And the graves were opened; and many bodies of the saints which slept arose, And came out of the graves after his resurrection, and went into the holy city, and appeared unto many." Various writers who observed this miraculous resurrection recorded the event. Jesus Christ had risen from the dead and won the victory over death, not only for Himself as the Son of God, but also for those saints who had died centuries before and for all who would believe in Him as their Lord and Savior in the centuries to follow. Many of the significant writings by Christians in the first three centuries were collected in a series of volumes called the *Ante-Nicene Library*. This library includes several ancient Christian manuscripts that mention the resurrection of saints described in Matthew 27:52–53. One of these manuscripts includes the claim that this resurrection involved "a great number, as it were, twelve thousand men, who had risen with the Lord." According to the ancient documents, these resurrected Old Testament saints walked through Israel for forty days, appeared to many people in Jerusalem, and then ascended with Jesus Christ when He ascended to His Father in Heaven.

It is no coincidence that Jesus Christ and these saints both arose on the seventeenth day of Nisan in A.D. 32, the day known as the Feast of the Firstfruits. Other notable events connected with the theme of resurrection also occurred on this anniversary. On this very same day the ark of Noah rested on Mount Ararat and the human race was resurrected following the flood. Almost a thousand years later, on this anniversary, Moses led the people of Israel through the Red Sea to be resurrected as a nation from the bondage of Egypt. Forty years later, Israel crossed the Jordan on the seventeenth day of Nisan, and the people enjoyed the firstfruits of the Promised Land. In the sovereignty of God, He caused Jesus Christ to rise from the dead and to bring these saints with Him into new life on this same day.

The passage in Matthew's gospel about the resurrection of the Old Testament saints is important because it illustrates Christ's power over death and sin to resurrect, not only Himself, but a whole group of believers in Him. We can learn several important things from examining this passage. Those who died before the resurrection of Christ experienced the same benefit of salvation from His atonement for our sins by His death on the cross as those who have lived since. Perhaps the most important lesson from this incident in the Gospels is that Jesus Christ conquered and disabled death by His triumphant death and resurrection. The saints that rose from the dead with Christ were the crowns of His victory over the power of death. When Jesus defeated the power of sin and death and "ascended up on high, he led captivity captive, and gave gifts unto men" (Ephesians 4:8). Christ's greatest gifts to mankind are salvation and the promise of resurrection and eternal life. This was His promise to Martha just before raising Lazarus from his grave. "Jesus said unto her, I am the resurrection, and the life: he that believeth in me, though he were dead, yet shall he live: And whosoever liveth and believeth in me shall never die. Believest thou this?" (John 11:25–26)

The message of Hebrews 11 awakened the Christians to their true hope, the heavenly city New Jerusalem, the final home of the Bride of Christ. In Hebrews, the Scriptures tell us that the Old Testament believers were motivated by their longing for the realization of the promises of God regarding His ultimate kingdom. Speaking of Abraham, Hebrews says, "For he looked for a city which hath foundations, whose builder and maker is God" (Hebrews 11:10). The writer further described the centrality of their longing for Heaven to their faith and hope with these inspired words: "These all died in faith, not having received the promises, but having seen them afar off, and were persuaded of them, and embraced them, and confessed that they were strangers and pilgrims on the earth. For they that say such things declare plainly that they seek a country" (Hebrews 11:13–14). The hope of physical resurrection from death was a fundamental truth taught throughout the Old Testament and was believed to be the promise of God to all those who loved and obeyed God.

The Promise of the Rapture

Christians today often speak about the Rapture, the miraculous moment when Christ will cause all living Christians to "rise to meet Him in the air." Although the word "rapture" does not appear in the English translations of the Bible, the concept is clearly taught in several different verses. It is worth remembering that the word "Trinity" also does not appear in the Bible, but the concept of a triune God is declared in many passages. The word Rapture comes from the Latin word "rapere," which means to "snatch away" or be "caught up." It is an excellent word to describe what the Bible declares will happen to all living saints who are alive at the moment when the "last trump" is blown and Christ calls His Church home to Heaven. The Rapture refers to the resurrection of the saints. Paul talks about this event in his first letter to the church at Thessalonica: "For the Lord Himself will descend from Heaven with a shout, with the voice of an archangel, and with the trumpet of God. . . . Then we who are alive . . . shall be caught up [raptured] . . . to meet the Lord in the air. And thus we shall always be with the Lord" (1 Thessalonians 4:16,17).

The Bible declares, "it is appointed unto men once to die, but after this the judgment" (Hebrews 9:27). However, there is one generation of Christians who will not experience physical death before entering Heaven — they will be raptured. They will pass from "life unto life" rather than from "death unto life." This will be the first generation in history that will escape the curse of death.

The First Teaching on the Rapture

The first teaching about the Rapture in the New Testament is found in the words of Jesus to His friend Martha after the death of her brother, Lazarus. "Then said Martha unto Jesus, Lord, if thou hadst been here, my brother had not died." Then Jesus assured her about the resurrection: "Jesus saith unto her, Thy brother shall rise again. Martha saith unto him, I know that he shall rise again in the resurrection at the last day. Jesus said unto her, I am the resurrection, and the life: he that believeth in me, though he were dead, yet shall he live. And whosoever liveth and believeth in me shall never die. Believest thou this" (John 11:21, 23–25).

For many years, when I read this passage in the gospel of John, I believed that Christ was simply repeating himself for emphasis in this last sentence. However, upon closer examination, I believe that this passage contains the first clear teaching in the New Testament about the Rapture of the Christians living in the generation when Christ returns. Notice that Jesus is talking about two distinct groups of believers. The first group to be raptured is made up of those believers who have already died, and will continue to die, during the period between the birth of the Church and the coming of Christ: "He that believeth in me, though he were dead, yet shall he live."

The second group to be resurrected are the believers alive at that event who are included in Jesus' second statement: "And whosoever liveth and believeth in me shall never die. Believest thou this?" (John 11:25). There will be a generation of believers who will not have to pass through death to reach eternal life, but who will be "caught up together to meet the Lord in the air" as Paul says in 1 Thessalonians. These believers who are alive on the day when Jesus Christ comes will be "caught up" physically, and their bodies will be transformed so that they are fit to live in Heaven forever with Christ.

This great promise of the coming resurrection was given to the Church by Jesus Christ and is affirmed by the apostle Paul:

> Behold, I show you a mystery; We shall not all sleep, but we shall all be changed, In a moment, in the twinkling of an eye, at the last trump: for the trumpet shall sound, and the dead shall be raised incorruptible, and we shall be changed. For this corruptible must put on incorruption, and this mortal must put on immortality. So when this corruptible shall have put on incorruption, and this mortal shall have put on immortality, then shall be brought to pass the saying that is written, Death is swallowed up in victory" (1 Corinthians 15:51–54).

In this passage, Paul confirms the revelation by Jesus that the Church had not previously understood about the coming of the Lord and the rapture of the living saints. Paul wrote his letter to the church at Corinth during his third missionary journey, probably during the winter of A.D. 55, twenty-three years after Jesus Christ taught His disciples about the events of the last days as recorded in Matthew 24. By this time, Jesus' disciples were traveling throughout the world as Jesus had commanded them, preaching all the things they had heard Jesus teach as they lived with Him during His years of ministry.

The Hope of the Second Coming

The Second Coming, including the rapture or "catching up" of the Church, was widely taught in the early Church. The early apostolic Church taught the prophetic truths about the pre-millennial return of Christ for hundreds of years. In my book, *Armageddon*, I quote from twelve early Church writers who share the same belief as the apostolic Church that Christ would return to the earth in glory before the Millennium. Although they did not use the English word "Rapture" to describe Christians being "caught up to meet Him in the air," they constantly warned believers to be watchful for the soon return of Christ. I have not found one theologian in the early church before A.D. 250 who denied the truth of the Rapture that was taught by Paul in 1 Thessalonians 4:13–18.

During the years leading to A.D. 300, several teachers began to teach a method of biblical interpretation that "spiritualized" many truths of the Bible. Led by Origen in Alexandria, Egypt, this liberal party gradually grew within the Church. They began to spiritualize and "allegorize" many biblical teachings, including the prophecies about the return of Christ and the Millennium. They denied the literal return of Jesus. They also denied that He was the Son of God.

As the Church fell under the influence of emperors like Constantine (A.D. 288–337), who supported Christianity, it began to take on political status. The belief in the actual return of Christ to set up His kingdom on earth quickly withered away. Naturally, a Roman emperor like Constantine did not look with favor on the biblical prophecy that all Gentile world empires would be overthrown by the Second Coming of Christ. Augustine (354–430), the most influential theologian since Paul, began to teach that the return of Christ, the Battle of Armageddon, and the Millennium were allegories to be understood only symbolically. In his influential book, *The City of God,* he denied a future Millennium with Christ's return and reign. Tragically, this denial of the Scriptures set the tone for the majority of Catholic and Protestant theologians for a thousand years, until the Protestant Reformation restored the Bible as the only source of true doctrine.

As the Church grew in political power, people accepted the belief that the Millennial Kingdom existed here and now, not when Christ returned. With few brief exceptions, the study of prophecy was, for the most part, ignored by church leaders during the Middle Ages until the time of the Reformation by Martin Luther in 1520.

The Timing of the Resurrection

What is the sequence of events concerning the resurrection and the Second Coming of Christ? Will the Church be raptured before the Great Tribulation begins? Many Christians believe that the Rapture will precede the Great Tribulation. Others believe that while there will be a Rapture, it may not happen until the return of Christ in glory at the Battle of Armageddon. Some doubt that the Rapture is taught by the Bible. Why should the Church be raptured, or to use the New Testament words, "be caught up together" to meet Christ in the air? Surely the answer to the first question is because the Bible says so. But, why should God resurrect the bodies of Christians?

If there was no Rapture in our future, then we would be forced to spend eternity as spirits, without a body. It is essential that all believers receive a new spiritual body at the resurrection to enable us to enjoy all that Christ has prepared for us in Heaven. We are promised rewards for our faithfulness to Christ, which include mansions in the New Jerusalem and crowns of gold. The book of Revelation tells us that all believers who comprise the bride of Christ are invited to join the Marriage Supper of the Lamb of God in Heaven following the Resurrection where we will eat and drink with Him. "Blessed are they which are called unto the marriage supper of the Lamb. And he saith unto me, These are the true sayings of God" (Revelation 19:9).

During the future Millennium and throughout eternity on the new earth, the resurrected saints will rule and reign with Christ. "Blessed and holy is he that hath part in the first resurrection: on such the second death hath no power, but they shall be priests of God and of Christ, and shall reign with him a thousand years" (Revelation 20:6). Obviously, we cannot participate in these activities unless we receive a resurrection body. Therefore, at the moment of His coming in the air, Jesus will transform the bodies of the living saints simultaneously as He resurrects the bodies of those in Heaven who died as believers. "The dead in Christ will rise first" indicates that the spirits of the Christians in Heaven will be the first believers to receive their new transformed bodies. During the Rapture, at the moment their spirits join their new spiritual bodies, "we which are alive and remain shall be caught up together with them in the clouds, to meet the Lord in the air: and so shall we ever be with the Lord" (1 Thessalonians 4:17). Then, all of the resurrected saints will return to Heaven with Christ to receive our rewards and mansions in joyful reunion with all of our loved ones forever.

Jesus' Command to Be Watchful

The New Testament tells us in many places to be watchful for the coming of the Son of Man. The net result of these passages is that faithful Christians have lived in a spiritually dynamic tension of not knowing just when the Lord will come to resurrect us. If Christ had clearly stated that His return would not be for more than nineteen hundred years, the Church might have lost its sense of urgency and mission. There might have been fewer missionaries who felt compelled to obey the Great Commission, "Go ye therefore, and teach all nations, baptizing them in the name of the Father, and of the Son, and of the Holy Ghost: Teaching them to observe all things whatsoever I have commanded you: and, lo, I am with you alway, even unto the end of the world. Amen" (Matthew 28:19–20).

The great outpouring of missionary and evangelistic efforts since A.D. 1800 came primarily from churches that believed strongly in the literal Second Coming of Christ and hoped fervently that it might happen in their lifetime. Far from hindering the urgency of the Gospel, the belief in the pre-millennial and imminent return of Christ has been the greatest motivation for Christians to "go into all the world and preach the gospel."

The Holy Spirit has, in a sense, kept us on our toes spiritually for two thousand years by refraining from telling us exactly when Christ will return. Jesus prophesied that no one would know the exact time. (See Matthew 24:36, 42, 44, 50; 25:13; Mark 13:32; Luke 12:40, 46.) If the Bible had included one simple statement about the exact sequence of events regarding the Rapture and the coming of Christ in glory to set up His kingdom, all confusion in this matter would have been removed forever. As a result, many excellent and sincere Bible teachers arrive at different conclusions regarding whether the Rapture will happen before the Great Tribulation or after, when Christ returns at the Battle of Armageddon.

The Early Church and the Hope of the Rapture

Many of those who reject the doctrine of the pretribulation Rapture have dogmatically asserted that this doctrine was never taught before A.D. 1830. Obviously, the truth or error of the pretribulation Rapture can only be determined by an appeal to the authority of Scripture. However, the writers who reject the pretribulation Rapture have confused many Christians with their mistaken assertion that "the Rapture can't be true because no one ever taught this doctrine in the first 1800 years of the Church." As an example, in *The Blessed Hope*, George E. Ladd wrote, "We can find no trace of pretribulationism in the early church; and no modern pretribulationist has successfully proved that this particular doctrine was held by any of the church fathers or students of the Word before the nineteenth century." In *The Incredible Cover-Up*, Dave MacPherson claimed that no one ever taught the pretribulation Rapture until a woman named Margaret MacDonald proclaimed it during a trance vision in A.D. 1830. He claimed that this was the origin of the theory of the Rapture. However, this assertion is false! The doctrine of the pretribulation Rapture is derived from the Scriptures and was taught by a number of people in the centuries before 1830. In my book *Final Warning*, I cite many Bible scholars who saw this doctrine in the New Testament passages and wrote about it in their commentaries. These scholars include Peter Jurieu (1697), Dr. John Gill (1748), and James MacKnight (1763).

After ten years of careful searching, I discovered a fascinating manuscript that proves that the doctrine of the pretribulation Rapture was taught in the early Church. Ephraem the Syrian (A.D. 306–373) was a major theologian of the early Church who lived in the city of Edessa, in Asia

(Turkey). His hymns are still used in the liturgy of the Eastern Orthodox Church and appear in the Post-Nicene Library (a collection of writings after the A.D. 325 Council of Nicea), but most of his commentaries were never translated into English from the original Latin. Ephraem's teaching on the Rapture was never published in English until I quoted it in *Final Warning*. This important manuscript reveals a literal principle of biblical interpretation. Ephraem believed in the pre-millennial return of Christ. However, his most important statement describes the pretribulational return of Christ to take His elect saints to Heaven to escape the coming tribulation. In addition, Ephraem describes an Antichrist who will rule a revived Roman empire, and a great tribulation of 1,260 days with a rebuilt temple and the Two Witnesses. Ephraem's text was called *On the Last Times, the Antichrist, and the End of the World*. His ten-section manuscript described the last days in chronological sequence, beginning with the Rapture, the seven-year tribulation, the three-and-a-half-year Great Tribulation as the last part of the seven-year tribulation period, and the tyranny of the Antichrist, followed by Christ's return at Armageddon. Significantly, in section 2, Ephraem wrote about the Rapture as an "imminent" event that will occur without warning: "We ought to understand thoroughly therefore, my brothers what is imminent or overhanging."

Ephraem then described the pretribulation Rapture as follows: "For all saints and the Elect of the Lord are gathered together before the tribulation which is about to come and are taken to the Lord in order that they may not see at any time the confusion which overwhelm the world because of our sins." Ephraem reminded his Christian readers that we need not fear the coming tribulation: "We neither become very much afraid of the report nor of the appearance . . ."

because the Rapture will occur prior to the tribulation that is coming. Further, Ephraem calls on Christians to "prepare ourselves for the meeting of the Lord Christ, so that He may draw us from the confusion, which overwhelms the world."

Ephraem described the "great tribulation" as lasting "three and a half years," precisely "1,260 days." He summarized, "There will be a great tribulation, as there has not been since people began to be upon the earth." In section 10 he wrote, "And when the three and a half years have been completed, the time of the Antichrist, through which he will have seduced the world, after the resurrection of the two prophets . . . will come the sign of the Son of Man, and coming forward the Lord shall appear with great power and much majesty." In another of his manuscripts, *The Book of the Cave of Treasures*, Ephraem revealed that the whole tribulation period encompassed "that sore affliction" lasting "one week" of seven years. He said that the 69th week of Daniel 9:24–27 ended with the crucifixion of Jesus. Although there are curious elements in Ephraem's manuscript, he clearly taught that the 70th week of Daniel's 70 Weeks was to be fulfilled in the final seven years of this age. "At the end of the world and at the final consummation. . . . After one week of that sore affliction (Tribulation), they will all be destroyed in the plain of Joppa. . . . Then will the son of perdition appear, of the seed and of the tribe of Dan."

This discovery of the 1600-year-old manuscript reveals that the doctrine of the blessed hope of resurrection and deliverance of the saints to Heaven prior to the Antichrist's reign was clearly held by some of the faithful at the beginning of the Church age. The full text of this important prophetic manuscript from the early Church can be read in my book *Final Warning*.

The extraordinary promise of God regarding our resurrection from death to live forever in the presence of Jesus Christ, our Lord and Savior, is breathtaking in its ability to lift the downtrodden soul and allow us to catch a glimpse of all that Jesus has prepared for those who love Him. Those who live in faith recognize that this life is only a foretaste of the eternal life in Heaven that our Lord has prepared for those who love Him.

The disciple John, who was especially beloved of the Lord, wrote about Christ's promise of resurrection for all who placed their faith in Him. "Marvel not at this: for the hour is coming, in the which all that are in the graves shall hear his voice, And shall come forth; they that have done good, unto the resurrection of life; and they that have done evil, unto the resurrection of damnation" (John 5:28–29).

The promise of Jesus Christ to His early followers about the final resurrection of all who place their faith and trust in Him remains our hope today:

> For the Lord himself shall descend from Heaven with a shout, with the voice of the archangel, and with the trump of God: and the dead in Christ shall rise first: Then we which are alive and remain shall be caught up together with them in the clouds, to meet the Lord in the air: and so shall we ever be with the Lord. Wherefore comfort one another with these words. (1 Thessalonians 4:16–18)

Notes

1. Blaise Pascal, *Pensees,* ed. A. J. Krailsheimer (London: Penguin Books, 1966).
2. *Westminster Confession of Faith* Chapter 32.
3. Voltaire, *Questions Concerning the Encyclopedia* Section 10.
4. J. H. Potts, *The Golden Dawn* (Philadelphia: P. W. Zeigler, 1884) 168.

10

The Testimony of Jesus About Hell

"Hell is an abiding place, but no resting place."
Thomas Watson

The Bible warns that today is "the day of salvation." As long as we are alive and until the day when Jesus Christ returns from Heaven to set up His earthly kingdom, we can still choose to turn from our sin and accept His offer of salvation. The apostle Paul proclaims God's promise of salvation to any whom will repent, but he also warns that God's offer will not be available forever. "For he saith, I have heard thee in a time accepted, and in the day of salvation have I succoured thee: behold, now is the accepted time; behold, now is the day of salvation" (2 Corinthians 6:2).

As surely as God declares that today is "the day of

salvation," He also warned that a day will finally arrive in the life of every man and woman when salvation's open door to Heaven will close forever. Then those who reject Christ face the inevitable prospect of an eternity in spiritual darkness in Hell. Jesus Himself announced the dreadful words of final judgment that will face everyone who in the end says, "No" to God's mercy. Christ warned, "Then shall he say also unto them on the left hand, Depart from me, ye cursed, into everlasting fire, prepared for the devil and his angels. And these shall go away into everlasting punishment: but the righteous into life eternal" (Matthew 25:41,46).

There is no question that Hell is a subject that most of us would like to avoid. Yet, if we truly desire to understand the nature of our life after death, we need to carefully examine the statements of Jesus about the ultimate destiny of those who refuse God's forgiveness and Heaven itself. The writer Thomas Watson once wrote, "The Scriptures tell us that in Hell there are these three things: there is darkness, there is fire, and there are chains."

Many years ago people used the curious expression, "a Hell, fire, and brimstone preacher," to describe a strong evangelical speaker who warned his listeners earnestly about the dangers of Hell. However, in our generation the preaching and teaching about the reality of Hell has virtually disappeared from seminaries, Bible colleges, and from many of the pulpits throughout the land. Prior to 1800 almost all pastors and theologians taught the reality of Hell as the eternal abode of all those who died without repenting of their sins. The great American preacher, Jonathan Edwards, delivered one of the most stirring and famous addresses of all time in the mid-1700s entitled "Sinners in the Hands of an Angry God." The literary qualities of his powerful message, combined with his graphic language depicting the horrors of an eternal Hell that awaited sinners who rejected God's salvation, caused this sermon to be studied for many decades by students of literature as well as theology. Reverend Jonathan Edwards declared:

> That world of misery, that lake of burning brimstone is extended abroad under you. There is the dreadful pit of the glowing flames of the wrath of God; there is Hell's wide gaping mouth open; and you have nothing to stand upon, nor any thing to take hold of; there is nothing between you and Hell but the air; tis only the power and mere pleasure of God that holds you up.

When Edwards preached his powerful sermon, thousands of sinners repented of their sinful ways and turned to God. The gradual abandonment of the teaching about Hell began in the pulpits of churches in Europe and America throughout the 1800s. This trend has continued until now only the conservative and evangelical churches in North America preach the warnings of Christ about Hell. Yet Jesus Christ Himself commanded us to "preach ye upon the house tops. And fear not them which kill the body, but are not able to kill the soul: but rather fear him which is able to destroy both soul and body in Hell" (Matthew 10:27–28). It is noteworthy that those churches that led the massive evangelical and missionary efforts during the last one hundred and fifty years usually emphasized the doctrines of both Heaven and Hell.

In our day, most Christians have never personally studied the Bible's warnings about the danger of Hell, nor have most people ever heard a biblically based sermon that warns about the absolute need to repent to escape it. Today, the average person in the Western world feels almost no real threat from the teaching about Hell. The word "Hell" has itself become almost a trivial expression during the last century to the point that many people comfortably use the word in casual curses without ever truly considering the terrible eternal reality that this word represents. In 1927 the well-known English atheist philosopher Bertrand Russell declared that many churchmen in his own day had already abandoned the traditional belief in the existence of Hell.[1] A 1990 poll by the Gallup organization reported that a surprising 66 percent of American Protestants and 57 percent of Catholics believed in the existence of Hell.[2]

Despite the fact that the majority of lay people in all denominations still believe in Hell, most theologians indicated that this was no longer true of them. Of the theologians surveyed, 66 percent of Protestant theologians and 39 percent of Catholic theologians expressed their disbelief in the doctrine of Hell.[3] The real question is this: Why have so many theologians, both liberal and some conservative, abandoned their belief in the Bible's teaching about Hell?

Obviously, the objection most people have with the doctrine is that they feel that an eternal Hell is morally indefensible. The problem of evil itself is inextricably tied up with the problem of Hell. There are many Christian laymen and pastors who find it difficult to reconcile the doctrine of an eternal Hell for unrepentant sinners with the concept of a holy and loving God. The thought of anyone experiencing eternal torment is extremely difficult to contemplate, even extremely wicked individuals such as Adolph Hitler, Joseph Stalin, or Mao Tse Tung, each of whom is morally responsible for millions of innocent victims being tortured and killed.

Nevertheless, Jesus Christ repeatedly confirmed that Hell would be the eternal destiny of those who reject His forgiveness of their sins. While some theologians have tried to distance themselves from this fact, the New Testament repeatedly records Jesus' teaching that His sacrificial death on the cross was the only acceptable price that could be paid for our deliverance. In his book *Providence and Evil,* theologian Peter Geach wrote, "We cannot be Christians, followers of Christ, we cannot even know what it is to be a Christian unless the Gospels give at least an approximately correct account of Christ's teaching. And if the Gospel account is even approximately correct, then it is perfectly clear that according to that teaching many men are irretrievably lost. . . ."[4]

The truth is that Christianity is inextricably entwined with Jesus Christ's teaching about His resurrection from the grave and its significance regarding our deliverance from an eternity in Hell. Many Christians realize that the doctrine of Hell is fundamental to the meaning of Christ's sacrificial death on the cross for our sins. In fact, if the doctrine of salvation from Hell is removed from Christianity, then the believer's acceptance of Christ as Savior is called into question. The core teaching of Christianity is that a sinful humanity has rebelled and separated itself from our holy Creator, God. Either we continue in our sinful rebellion against God, inevitably leading us to an eternity in Hell, or we repent of our sins by accepting Christ's sacrificial death on the cross in our place so that we might be reconciled to God in Heaven forever. The author Pedro Calderon de la Barca once wrote about our final destiny as follows: "Tis not where we lie, but whence we fell: The loss of heaven's the greatest pain in Hell."[5]

However, for those theologians and others who reject

the reality of Hell as the alternative to Christ's offer of salvation in Heaven, Christianity has become somewhat reduced into a new philosophy, an alternative life style, or a new religious self-image.

The evangelist Charles Reign Scoville once declared, "If Hell were nothing but eternal homesickness, it would still be Hell." In this simple statement, Reverend Scoville acknowledged that the loss of our loved ones, and the loss of our home, work, and friends, would truly be a part of Hell. However, those who truly love Jesus Christ die in faith, knowing that all of these things will be restored forever in Heaven.

While there are many things about Hell that have been hidden from humans, the Bible declares that Hell is absolutely real and that it will last forever. The reality of the punishment of Hell is affirmed in numerous verses throughout the Scriptures. "He that believeth and is baptized shall be saved; but he that believeth not shall be damned" (Mark 16:16). The Scriptures repeatedly affirm that those who reject God's salvation will endure an eternity in Hell where they will experience "fire and brimstone." In Revelation 14:10 John wrote, "The same shall drink of the wine of the wrath of God, which is poured out without mixture into the cup of his indignation; and he shall be tormented with fire and brimstone in the presence of the holy angels, and in the presence of the Lamb." Jesus warned the people listening to Him to turn away from their sins to escape the "furnace of fire." Matthew recorded this terrible warning by Jesus: "And shall cast them into a furnace of fire: there shall be wailing and gnashing of teeth" (Matthew 13:42).

Aside from the terrors of Hell itself, one of the most horrible things endured by those in Hell will be the knowledge that they have freely chosen to refuse Christ's forgiveness and His offer of the glorious "kingdom of God." The apostle Paul warned, "Know ye not that the unrighteous shall not inherit the kingdom of God?" (1 Corinthians 6:9). Some theologians have tried valiantly to escape the teaching of the Scriptures about the terrors of Hell by suggesting that Hell might be the total annihilation of the sinner's soul, or at least a lack of consciousness about his condition throughout eternity. The Scriptures, however, clearly state that those who reject Christ's mercies during this life will endure an eternity in Hell while fully conscious forever. Jesus said, "But the children of the kingdom shall be cast out into outer darkness: there shall be weeping and gnashing of teeth" (Matthew 8:12). It is hard to say whether the physical torments of Hell will be worse than the spiritual pain of contemplating an eternity cut off from light, love, and peace in a place filled with equally unrepentant sinners.

A Description of Hell

The Scriptures declare that Hell is a real place, though perhaps in another dimension from this earth. Three different words are used throughout the Bible to describe Hell. The first word, *hades,* describes the spiritual place of waiting where departed spirits were held after death. However, before the resurrection of Jesus Christ, hades was divided into two portions that were separated by a great impassible gulf. On one side of hades was Abraham's Bosom, which held the souls of all those saints who had died with faith in God during the Old Testament period until the time of the resurrection of Christ (Luke 16:23). Those souls in Abraham's Bosom were conscious in a pleasant place of waiting until Jesus Christ descended into hades after His death on the cross to "preach to the spirits in prison" (I

Peter 3:19). When these departed saints of the Old Testament finally heard the words of Jesus, the Son of God, they could understand fully for the first time what they had only faithfully perceived in part, since they had no knowledge of Jesus Christ's future role in God's plan of salvation. However, those unrighteous souls who rejected their conscience and whatever part of God's truth that was presented to them went to the part of hades known as the place of "torment."

Another Greek word, *Tartarus*, is translated as Hell, and appears in only one passage of Scripture. "For if God spared not the angels that sinned, but cast them down to Hell, and delivered them into chains of darkness, to be reserved unto judgment" (2 Peter 2:4). This passage indicates that there is a special part of Hell in which God imprisoned those fallen angels who chose to defile mankind in the ancient past before the Flood by having illicit sexual relations with the women of earth (Genesis 6:1–5). Their great sin was the violation of God's prohibition by breaking the physical barrier between angels and mankind through forbidden illicit sexual relations. The book of Jude reveals the nature of these fallen angels' sins at the dawn of man's existence on the earth. "And the angels which kept not their first estate, but left their own habitation, he hath reserved in everlasting chains under darkness unto the judgment of the great day" (Jude 6).

The final word repeatedly translated as Hell in the Bible is the word *Gehenna*, a word that occurs in many passages, such as Matthew 5:22–30 and Mark 9:43–47. For example, in Matthew 5:22 we read these words, "Whosoever shall say, Thou fool, shall be in danger of Hell fire." Gehenna was the name of the horrible, open, burning garbage pit whose fire and incredible stench never ceased in the Valley of Hinnom, just outside the city walls of Jerusalem. Gehenna was the place where the Jews threw their garbage and the bodies of criminals to rot and burn. Significantly, Jesus Himself used the word gehenna to describe Hell in each of twelve passages in the New Testament where the word Hell appears.

The poet Will Carleton once wrote, "To appreciate Heaven well, Tis good for a man to have some fifteen minutes of Hell."[6] The well-respected founder of the Salvation Army, William Booth declared that he wished his Christian workers could observe the terrors of Hell for a few minutes to properly motivate them to preach salvation to a world of sinners.

The Degrees of Punishment in Hell

Are there degrees of punishment for sinners in Hell, or will all sinners experience the same eternal punishment regardless of their personal sins and wickedness? The holiness and justice of God demands that there will be different degrees of punishment that will accurately reflect the different evil deeds and motives of those who reject Christ's forgiveness: "Shall not the Judge of all the earth do right?" (Genesis 18:25). God's holiness demands that He will wisely, justly, and correctly judge each sinner.

The apostle John wrote of the final judgment of sinners:

> And I saw a great white throne, and him that sat on it, from whose face the earth and the Heaven fled away; and there was found no place for them. And I saw the dead, small and great, stand before God; and the books were opened: and another book was opened, which is the book of life: and the dead were judged out of those things which were written in the books, according to their works. And the sea gave up the

> dead which were in it; and death and Hell delivered up the dead which were in them: and they were judged every man according to their works. And death and Hell were cast into the lake of fire. This is the second death. (Revelation 20:11–14)

Since every single person who appears at this judgment before the throne of God in Heaven is an unrepentant sinner, there would be no need for judgment unless individual sentences were to be handed out by man's final judge, God Almighty. Notice that the "books" containing God's permanent record of men's deeds will be "opened" and "they were judged every man according to their works." The Judge of all the earth will condemn the evil deeds of Adolph Hitler more harshly than He will judge a woman who lived a good life, but failed to accept Christ. Yet both unrepentant souls will endure an unimaginable eternity in Hell forever because they rejected the only hope of salvation ever offered by God to atone for our sins.

Christ taught that God would judge the sins of each individual, His parable about faithfulness and watchfulness (Luke 12:35–48). He also implied that there will be differences in the punishment of those in Hell when He condemned the sinful deeds of some hypocritical religious leaders. "Woe unto you, scribes and Pharisees, hypocrites! for ye devour widows' houses, and for a pretence make long prayer: therefore ye shall receive the greater damnation" (Matthew 23:14). His warning of "greater damnation" teaches that God's judgment of individual souls, based on their deeds and motives, will properly reflect their sins and guilt. Jesus Christ has already paid the sacrificial price for our sins. The great tragedy is that millions of people choose not to reap the benefits of His sacrifice.

The Evil Company Who Will Inhabit Hell

We have all heard people foolishly joke that when they die and go to Hell, they will hold a great party because all of their friends will be there as well. These careless jokes reflect the almost total absence of belief in the reality and the horror of an eternity in Hell. The Bible describes Hell as "a lake of fire" that burns forever. Unrepentant sinners will have a resurrected body that cannot be destroyed. Jesus warned, "And if thine eye offend thee, pluck it out: it is better for thee to enter into the kingdom of God with one eye, than having two eyes to be cast into Hell fire. Where their worm dieth not, and the fire is not quenched" (Mark 9:47). One of the most terrible things about Hell is that the resurrected bodies of unrepentant sinners will never die. "And whosoever was not found written in the book of life was cast into the lake of fire" (Revelation 20:15).

Yet consider for a moment the companions who will share Hell with those who stubbornly resist God's mercy to the very end — Hitler, Stalin, plus every other murderer and torturer in history. Hell will be filled forever with untold billions of angry sinners who will still possess bodies that can feel pain, but can never die. In their pain and rage against God's justice, these angry sinners will curse God and each other. Their evil desire will be to revenge themselves on God, but they cannot succeed. It is more than likely that they will exact revenge for their punishment on their companions in Hell.

Consider for one horrible moment what a normal citizen would experience if they were condemned to live in the worst penitentiary in North America, totally at the mercy of the wicked, perverted prisoners. Imagine that there were no guards or cell bars to protect you from the rage and cruelty of the merciless criminals who shared your jail. The only mercy you could hope for would be a swift death. However, those who reject the salvation of Jesus Christ to the very end of their lives will face a situation far more horrible than the one just suggested. Those who reject Christ's forgiveness will have chosen to spend their eternity in Hell with every unrepentant murderer, rapist, pervert, torturer, and vile person who ever lived. Those sinners who tormented their fellow citizens while on earth will not suddenly change their behavior for the better when they are imprisoned forever in Hell with no hope of release for good behavior. In light of the horrors that will inevitably be connected to the terrible, enraged companions in Hell, God's warning about the "lake of fire," the "darkness," "weeping," and "gnashing of teeth" provide each of us with a strong motive to discover how we may obtain Christ's forgiveness and salvation so that we may enjoy Heaven throughout eternity.

God's Justice and Hell

Human nature naturally tends to minimize both the evil and horror of our sinful rebellion against our Creator and sinful actions against our family, associates, and neighbors. God created humanity to live in perfect love and harmony with each other and our Creator. However, at the very first opportunity, Adam and Eve rejected the laws of God regarding their behavior in the Garden of Eden. They consciously chose to follow the deceptive temptation of Satan to become "as gods, knowing good and evil" (Genesis 3:1–7). The Lord had warned them against disobedience to His laws in that "in the day that thou eatest thereof, thou shalt surely die" (Genesis 2:17). However, Satan, the great liar, lied to Eve when he assured her, "Ye shall not surely die" (Genesis 3:4).

When Adam and Eve rebelled, they died spiritually as God had promised. As a result, every human born after the Fall of Adam and Eve also experienced spiritually death as a result of their spiritual rebellion against God. Until the moment of Adam and Eve's rebellious sin, no living being on earth had ever experienced death. When our first parents rebelled against the command of their loving Father, they created an enormous barrier that prevented their entrance into the holy presence of God. God is perfectly holy, just, and without sin. Just as a light naturally banishes darkness from a room, God's perfect holiness makes it simply impossible for sin and evil to exist in His sinless presence. When a sinner sincerely asks God for forgiveness, Jesus covers and atones for their sins. When Jesus Christ judicially took upon Himself the sins of the world (2 Corinthians 5:21), God then accepted the sacrificial death of Christ as the full judicial payment for all of man's rebellion and sin. "As far as the Heaven is high above the earth, and as far as the east is from the west, so far hath He removed our transgressions from us" (Psalms 103:12–12). Those who repent of their sinful rebellion and ask for His forgiveness will receive God's complete pardon for their rebellion that was purchased with the blood of Christ at Calvary.

However, those who reject their personal need for Christ's forgiveness seem to expect that God has abolished His Word, and eliminated the need for divine justice. They seem to think that God will allow unrepentant sinners to escape Hell and enter Heaven, despite the obvious fact that they openly reject Jesus' claim to be the Son of God and their Savior. However, if God allowed unrepentant sinners into Heaven, that part of the heavenly city would immediately be polluted by their evil presence. This sinfully polluted portion of the city would be transformed into a corner of Hell.

Consider for a moment about the natural reaction of average non-Christians if they were to find themselves in the midst of a Christian spiritual retreat focused on worship of Jesus Christ. A non-Christian would likely panic and flee from association with Christians who love and worship God. Consider the hypothetical situation if an unrepentent, Christ-hating sinner would enter Heaven. How would they react? Living in the heavenly City of God would not be "heavenly" for them. An unrepentent sinner would hate Heaven and despise all of the inhabitants of the New Jerusalem. Therefore, it is clear that just as light drives out the darkness in our physical world, the sinless holiness of God will make it absolutely impossible for an unrepentant sinner to enter Heaven or to experience the glory of the heavenly city unless their sins were washed away forever by the sacrificial death of Jesus Christ on the Cross.

The Duration of Hell

The writer Thomas Brooks described the awful duration of Hell as follows: "The damned shall live as long in Hell as God Himself shall live in Heaven." Many liberal theologians who accept the scriptural reality of Hell still seek to minimize its horrors. They suppose that those who enter Hell will finally emerge at some point of time in the future and take their place in Heaven among the blessed of the Lord. Some suggest that the Bible really intended to communicate the idea of the total annihilation of the souls of those who finally reject Christ's salvation rather than the condemnation of these souls to an eternity without end in Hell.

The Scriptures reveal that Hell will last forever and that the souls who reject Christ's mercy will not be annihilated but will be conscious forever. The poet John Webster wrote about the dreadful eternal nature of Hell: "That's the greatest torture souls feel in Hell: In Hell, that they must live, and cannot die."[7] Liberal philosophers and modern theologians who deny that God created man in His image now dare to create a god in their own image. They suggest that, if only God were more like their humanistic image of Him, He would be compassionate and never send men and women to an eternity in Hell. What these theologians fail to understand is that God is not only far more loving and compassionate than we can ever understand, but He is also absolutely just and holy. His overwhelming love and compassion motivated God to send His only-begotten Son, Jesus Christ, to die on the Cross to bear full punishment for the sins of mankind. However, His absolute holiness and justice demands that, if men still choose to reject His blood-bought pardon, then they must themselves bear the eternal consequences of their sinful rejection of God and His salvation. The just and holy consequence of unrepentant sin is Hell. Paul declared, "the wages of sin is death." (Romans 6:23)

The New Testament Scriptures use the Greek word αιωυας, which is translated by the English word "forever" more than thirty times by the King James Version translators to describe the duration of the soul's experience in Hell. It is significant that even a theologian who rejects the conclusion of Hell's eternity was forced to admit that twenty-nine of the thirty references to Hell cannot possibly be interpreted as anything other than "forever" or "eternally" in the normal sense of the language.[8] In fact, it is significant that the same Greek words used to describe the eternal duration of Hell are used in other passages of the Bible to describe the eternal duration of our experience and enjoyment of heaven's glories (Jude v. 7 and 2 Peter 1:11). Numerous other examples can be examined in any good Greek-English concordance on the New Testament.

The concept of eternity is almost impossible for the human mind to completely grasp. The nature of our mind and our daily experience in this temporal life make it virtually impossible to conceive of a life that continues forever without an end. However, the Puritan writer Thomas Watson wrote about the terrible reality of a Hell that will never ever end. "The torments of Hell abide for ever. . . . If all the earth and sea were sand, and every thousandth year a bird should come, and take away one grain of sand, it would be a long time ere that vast heap of sand were emptied; yet, if after all that time the damned may come out of Hell, there were some hope; but this word *EVER* breaks the heart."

Finally, we need to consider what motive Jesus would have to die in agony on the Cross to enable sinners to escape Hell if its punishment was only of limited duration? It defies common sense that God would have sent His Son Jesus to endure the sacrifice of crucifixion if He knew that sinners would eventually survive a period of limited punishment in Hell and thereby qualify for life in Heaven, despite their rejection of Christ's sacrificial death. The truth that is declared from Genesis to Revelation is that Hell is horribly real, and that it will last forever. That is why it is so important that people turn from their sins while there is still time to repent and find salvation through personal faith in Jesus Christ, who makes this promise to every man: "Behold, I stand at the door and knock: if any man hear my voice, and open the door, I will come in to him, and will sup with him, and he with me" (Revelation 3:20).

Notes

1. Bertrand Russell, *Why I Am Not A Christian* (New York: Simon & Schuster, 1977).
2. "Hell's Sober Comeback," *U.S. News and World Report* March 1991.
3. "The IEA/Roper Center Theology Faculty Survey," *This World* 2 (1982): 50.
4. Peter T. Geach, *Providence and Evil* (Cambridge: Cambridge University Press, 1977) 123-124.
5. Pedro Calderon de la Barca, *Adventures of Five Hours* Act V.
6. Will Carleton, "Gone With a Handsomer Man," *Farm Ballads.*
7. John Webster, *Duchess of Malfi* Act IV, section 1,1.84.
8. Oxenham, *What is Truth as to Everlasting Punishment?* 101.

11

Heaven: The Greatest Promise Ever Made

> And God shall wipe away all tears from their eyes; and there shall be no more death, neither sorrow, nor crying, neither shall there be any more pain: for the former things are passed away. And he that sat upon the throne said, Behold, I make all things new. And he said unto me, Write: for these words are true and faithful. (Revelation 21:4–5)

God has not left us in darkness regarding our ultimate spiritual destiny. Jesus Christ revealed the truth about the nature of our new body, and many details about our ultimate destiny — Heaven or Hell.

From the time I was a young child, Heaven and the afterlife has held great fascination for me. This somewhat unusual curiosity began at a very early age when I first learned that my brother Bruce had died the year before I was born. Naturally I asked my parents where my brother was and what he would be doing each day. I can still remember them explaining to me about the wonders of Heaven, the glory of God's throne, and the beauty of the angels. My mother would open her Bible and teach me the tremendous promises of God about our heavenly home. The best promise of all is the final reunion at the Rapture that will bring together the souls of all those who have departed and all living saints.

One of the strongest impressions I still remember from our conversations is the unshakable confidence we share in the unbreakable prophecies of Christ about the heavenly mansions He has prepared for those who place their faith and truth in Him. These conversations implanted an absolute conviction in me that our life does not end at death and that there is nothing to fear from death for those who place their trust in Christ. Although I have come perilously close to death several times, as a result of serious accidents and numerous operations, I have never been afraid of death because of my strong faith in Christ's promises about Heaven.

Jesus declared, "In my Father's house are many mansions: if it were not so, I would have told you. I go to prepare a place for you. And if I go and prepare a place for you, I will come again, and receive you unto myself; that where I am, there ye may be also" (John 14:2–3). The sincere longing for the heavenly city in the hearts of believers found its expression in glowing descriptions of Heaven, as revealed in moving hymns, sermons, stained glass windows, and countless books.

Throughout most of the last two thousand years,

during times when living conditions and the threat of religious persecution made life exceedingly difficult for most Christians, the Bible's promise of heaven's rest, its peace, and its glory at the end of a faithful life was welcome news. However, many Christians living today in North America and Europe share a life style of great comfort and wealth beyond anything our forefathers could have imagined. In light of the great improvements in our life style, health care, and civil rights, the subject of our future heavenly home has been supplanted in the hearts of many Christians by a new focus on spiritual experiences, healing ministries, and promises of prosperity.

In contrast to this unbalanced focus on earthly concerns, Jesus Christ repeatedly told His disciples to turn their thoughts and concerns toward spiritual and heavenly matters and not to concentrate unduly upon the temporary events and material things of this passing life. When the rich young ruler asked Jesus the question, "Master, what shall I do that I may inherit eternal life?" Jesus replied, "One thing thou lackest: go thy way, sell whatsoever thou hast, and give to the poor, and thou shalt have treasure in Heaven: and come, take up the cross, and follow me" (Mark 10:21). Jesus warned that being religious was not the key to the gates of Heaven: "Not every one that saith unto me, Lord, Lord, shall enter into the kingdom of Heaven; but he that doeth the will of my Father which is in Heaven"(Matthew 7:21).

In another passage, Christ addressed the very temporary nature of our earthly treasures and rewards which quickly pass away. Jesus encouraged believers to follow Him and to win the glorious reward of "treasures in Heaven," which will be cherished and enjoyed with our loved ones forever. "But lay up for yourselves treasures in Heaven, where neither moth nor rust doth corrupt, and where thieves do not break through nor steal" (Matthew 6:20). If we faithfully "take up our cross" in our daily walk and keep our eyes focused on the final goal of Heaven, Jesus promises that our faithfulness to Him will be eternally rewarded when we finally stand before the Throne of God.

The writer of the book of Hebrews reminds believers of the true value of the eternal treasures and rewards awaiting those who remain faithful. "For ye had compassion of me in my bonds, and took joyfully the spoiling of your goods, knowing in yourselves that ye have in Heaven a better and an enduring substance" (Hebrews 10:34). Millions of believers have sacrificed their possessions, their employment, their homes, and their freedom rather than deny their faith in Jesus Christ.

A Longing For Heaven

Who seeks for Heaven alone to save his soul
May keep the path, but will not reach the goal;
While he who walks in love may wander far,
Yet God will bring him where the blessed are.[1]

This poem by Henry van Dyke reminds us that God's nature is characterized by pure love and mercy toward those in need. God measures and rewards our spirit in terms of the love we possess and manifest to those around us. If we do not express love for our fellow human beings by sharing with them our faith, our assistance, and our possessions, it is because the love of Christ has not yet penetrated our heart. While Heaven often seems so distant due to the constant distractions of our daily life, God has implanted a supernatural longing for our heavenly home within the heart of every man or woman who freely yields their spirit to Him. This longing was expressed by Paul Lawrence Dunbar:

"There is a Heaven, for ever, day by day. The upward longing of my soul doeth tell me so."[2] This profound yearning expresses something far beyond our earthly perceptions and has the power to transform our spirit. William Shakespeare wrote, "The love of Heaven makes one heavenly."

Martin Luther, the great reformer who was instrumental in returning the Body of Christ, the true Church of God, to its true foundation based on the unchanging doctrines revealed in the Holy Scriptures, often expressed this deep longing for Heaven. The Reformer wrote about his appreciation of the true value of God's heavenly promises: "I would not give one moment of Heaven for all the joy and riches of the world, even if it lasted for thousands and thousands of years."

Someone once wrote that "everyone wants to go to Heaven, but no one wants to die." However, there are many people who have such a profound hatred of God and of His holiness that they would actually prefer to go to Hell than to endure the goodness and holiness of Heaven. In 1657, Reverend Richard Baxter wrote a powerful study of the reality of Heaven called *The Saints' Everlasting Res*t in which he said the following: "There is a great deal of difference between the desires of Heaven in a sanctified man and an unsanctified man. The believer prizeth it above earth, and had rather be with God than here. But to the ungodly, there is nothing seemeth more desirable than this world; and therefore he only chooseth Heaven before Hell, but not before earth; and therefore shall not have it upon such a choice"[3] While Baxter's language is quaint, his deep insight into the human motives that affect our eternal choices is quite sound. The brilliant preacher, Henry Ward Beecher, also wrote about the heart's desire in relation to our final destiny: "Heaven will be the endless portion of every man who has Heaven in his soul." In other words, if you do not truly and earnestly desire Heaven while you are in this world, you are unlikely to enjoy the heavenly city in the next world.

The great religious writer John Newton had lived an evil life as captain of a slave ship and was marvelously converted to follow Christ. Newton once wrote about his expectations about what would happen following his death: "If ever I reach Heaven I expect to find three wonders there: first, to meet some I had not thought to see there: second, to meet some I had expected to see there; and third, the greatest wonder of all, to find myself there." While the desire to enter Heaven after death is natural, it is vital that our concern for the souls of our friends, loved ones, and neighbors motivate us to share our faith in Christ with them now. Centuries ago Reverend Thomas Fuller wrote about the need for believers to possess a powerful passion for the salvation of others. He stated, "He will never get to Heaven who desire to go thither alone."[4]

Far from the inactivity that many imagine, we will find that Heaven is a truly great adventure. Tragically, because of the general lack of biblically based teaching about our future life in eternity, many Christians have a vague and misinformed vision of a somewhat boring Heaven where we will be engaged in the occasional harp lesson and stroll on the "streets of gold." Following the Rapture, every believer will enjoy using the awesome intellectual and supernatural abilities of our powerful new resurrection bodies. We will be able to travel from Heaven to earth at the speed of thought, as Jesus Himself did following His resurrection. The Gospels record that Jesus took with Him to Paradise the repentant thief from the Cross, the same day the Lord was crucified.

Jesus Christ prophesied, "And Jesus said unto him,

Verily I say unto thee, To day shalt thou be with me in Paradise"(Luke 23:43). The resurrected saints will enjoy wonderful friendships with both the biblical saints we have read about for so many years, as well as the millions of believers who have died since the time of Christ. Scientists estimate that most of us utilize less than ten percent of the potential mental abilities of our wondrously complex mind. Can you imagine what you would do if you were able to actualize the total memory and intellect that God originally gave humanity? After our resurrection, we will be able to study and master every single subject that attracts our interest throughout eternity.

In addition to enjoying the glories of God's heavenly city, the New Jerusalem, the saints will have access to the earth to enjoy her wholesome pleasures and participate in the Messiah's benevolent rule of the earth's population of both Jews and Gentiles. We will "rule and reign" with Him. Far from the complacent heavenly existence that most Christians have been taught, the Scriptures assure us that the saints will rule over the population of the hundreds of nations on the renovated earth forever. The prophet John tells us that the Lord has "made us kings and priests to our God; and we shall reign on the earth" (Revelation 5:10).

The New Jerusalem, the heavenly city, will be our eternal home. However we will still be able to travel to the earth to enjoy the wonders of nature and the beautiful variety that Christ created on this planet. In the book of Revelation the prophet John wrote, "Blessed and holy is he that hath part in the first resurrection: on such the second death hath no power, but they shall be priests of God and of Christ, and shall reign with him a thousand years" (Revelation 20:6). Revelation also reveals that after the one-thousand-year

Millennium concludes, we will rule the population of earth under the Messiah Jesus Christ forever. John wrote, "and they shall reign for ever and ever" (Revelation 22:5). The people on earth who will be ruled by the Messiah and His saints will be the one-third portion of humanity who will survive the terrible judgments, wars, and plagues of the Tribulation period and the cataclysmic Battle of Armageddon. The billions who survive will represent every nation of Gentiles and Jews. These survivors, and their descendents, will multiply to repopulate the earth.

The saints will join in the glorious and eternal worship of our Savior Jesus Christ, in the presence of hundreds of millions of angels. John wrote about his prophetic vision of Heaven in the book of Revelation: "Then I looked, and I heard the voice of many angels around the throne, the living creatures, and the elders; and the number of them was ten thousand times ten thousand, and thousands of thousands, saying with a loud voice: 'Worthy is the Lamb who was slain to receive power and riches and wisdom, and strength and honor and glory and blessing!'" (Revelation 5:11–12). Can you imagine joining your own voice to that celestial choir of angels and saints, in praise to Jesus, the King of Kings and Lord of Lords?

The mystery of Heaven is expressed by the apostle Paul in his letter to the church at Corinth: "But as it is written: 'Eye has not seen, nor ear heard, nor have entered into the heart of man the things which God has prepared for those who love Him'" (1 Corinthians 2:9). This verse correctly describes the inability of man to perceive the infinite wonders of Heaven using his own limited intellect and imagination. However, Paul prophesied that God would soon reveal additional truth about Heaven through His Holy Spirit. "But God has revealed them to us through His Spirit. For the Spirit searches all things, yes, the deep things of God" (1 Corinthians 2:10). Thirty years later the prophet John was inspired by God to record his incredible visions about the wonders of Heaven and the New Jerusalem. In the book of Revelation, John described his inspired vision of the heavenly life that awaits all believers. John was filled with wonder by his vision of the glorious heavenly city, the New Jerusalem, that will descend from Heaven to the new earth once this planet is restored from the ancient curse of sin and death.

> And I heard a loud voice from Heaven saying, 'Behold, the tabernacle of God is with men, and He will dwell with them, and they shall be His people, and God Himself will be with them and be their God. And God will wipe away every tear from their eyes; there shall be no more death, nor sorrow, nor crying; and there shall be no more pain, for the former things have passed away.' Then He who sat on the throne said, 'Behold, I make all things new.' And He said to me, 'Write, for these words are true and faithful.' (Revelation 21:3–5)

In the end we can only fully understand the Bible's revelations about Heaven through faith and trust in the written revelation of Christ. The book of Hebrews (11:1) tells us, "Now faith is the substance of things hoped for, the evidence of things not seen." We cannot know anything specific about the nature of our immortal existence in Heaven except for what God chooses to reveal about Himself and His eternal plan in the Holy Scriptures. Fortunately, Jesus and the New Testament prophets revealed many details about our future life in Heaven that had not been previously revealed to the Old Testament Church.

God promised that our lives in Heaven would be exciting

and challenging beyond our fondest dreams. There are several provocative hints in the Scriptures that suggest that many of the glorious wonders of creation that we find on earth were created from God's original blueprint in Heaven. For example, Moses was commanded to create the various worship implements, such as the Ark of the Covenant (Exodus 25:40) for the Tabernacle after the pattern or blueprint of the original worship items found in the heavenly Temple of God (Revelation 11:19). Moses recorded God's command, "According to all that I show thee, after the pattern of the tabernacle, and the pattern of all the instruments thereof, even so shall ye make it" (Exodus 25:9). The English poet John Milton wrote about this same possibility, "What if earth, Be but the shadow of Heaven, and things therein, Each to each other like, more than on earth is thought?"[5] The poet William Blake wrote about the nature of Heaven as follows, "There exist in that eternal world the permanent realities of every thing which we see reflected in this vegetable glass of nature."[6]

It is interesting to note that God gave King David the plans for the Temple that Solomon would eventually build in Jerusalem, apparently patterned after the original Temple in Heaven (1 Chronicles 28:1–12,19). The Scriptures declare that God created humanity "in the image of God." Genesis records, "And God said, 'Let us make man in our image, after our likeness'" (Genesis 1:26, 28; James 3:9). In light of these examples, and the intriguing descriptions in Revelation of cities, walls, thrones, the river of life, the tree of life, fruit, etcetera, Heaven will be much more real than most expect.

Promise of Heavenly Mansions

The ancient creeds of the Church affirm "that the chief end of man is to glorify God and enjoy Him forever." While these words may seem strange and foreign to our ears, they are the standard that the Bible itself sets for us. "Whether you eat or drink, or whatever you do; do all to the glory of God." Our goal as Christians is to know God as He knows us. The heavenly promises of God are staggering in their tremendous richness and variety. Perhaps this overwhelming list of promises has caused men to withdraw in disbelief. Yet the promises in the Word of God are unbreakable, despite the changing tides of religious fashion and doctrinal emphasis. Christ's invitation is: "Come, you blessed of My Father, inherit the kingdom prepared for you from the foundation of the world" (Matthew 25:34). In the midst of all our worldly pursuits and interests it is sometimes easy to forget that this life is simply a testing ground, a place of training for the wonders of our eternal life with Christ. The English writer Sir Thomas Moore wrote, "Earth has no sorrow that Heaven cannot heal."[7]

Although we cannot fully understand the richness of His promises, we must in faith accept and believe His words. For the Word tells us that "without faith it is impossible to please God." To be a follower of Christ we must believe by faith, live by faith, and walk by faith. Today, most people believe only those things that they can see with their own eyes. Yet the paradox of the Christian life is that we are commanded to believe first. At first, the disciple Thomas did not believe the prophecies of Jesus' death and resurrection. In mercy, Christ appeared to Thomas face to face and let him put his hand into His wounds to prove to him that He had truly risen from the dead. However, Jesus said, "Thomas, because you have seen Me, you have believed: blessed are those who have not seen, and yet have believed" (John 20:29).

John reveals God's purpose in giving us a written revelation of His truth in the Bible: "But these are written that you may believe that Jesus is the Christ, the Son of God, and that believing you may have life in His name" (John 20:31). After the wonderful miracle of the loaves and fishes the people anxiously followed Christ and asked, "What shall we do, that we may work the works of God?" Jesus answered and said to them, "This is the work of God, that you believe in Him whom He sent" (John 6:28–29). Jesus continued, "For I have come down from Heaven, not to do My own will, but the will of Him who sent Me. And this is the will of Him who sent Me, that everyone who sees the Son and believes in Him may have everlasting life; and I will raise him up at the last day" (John 6:38,40).

Most people would agree that true justice does not exist in this world. Life on earth, with its unresolved complexities, never seems completely fair. As the writer of the ancient book of Job stated, "the wicked often prosper and the good often suffer evil." However, both vision and intuition have convinced man there must be something beyond. We all hope for a day in which justice will be finally realized.

Anyone who realizes that our souls are eternal should find the subject of where we will spend eternity of supreme importance. Christians, those who have become the "sons of God through faith in Christ Jesus" (Galatians 3:26), are promised an eternal life where "we shall always be with the Lord" (1 Thessalonians 4:17). But what is the nature of the life we shall live and the mansions we shall enjoy? How will life in the City of God, the New Jerusalem, differ from our normal life on earth? Surely, it is essential that we study what God's Word has to tell us about the Holy City, the New

Jerusalem. In the final chapter we will explore in detail the phenomenal prophecies that Jesus foretold about living in the City of God, the New Jerusalem.

The Lord Himself promised His disciples that He would prepare a heavenly city for them and that He would return to take them to their eternal home.

> Let not your heart be troubled: ye believe in God, believe also in me. In my Father's house are many mansions: if it were not so, I would have told you. I go to prepare a place for you. And if I go and prepare a place for you, I will come again, and receive you unto myself; that where I am, there ye may be also. (John 14:1–3)

> And he saith unto me, Seal not the sayings of the prophecy of this book: for the time is at hand. (Revelation 22:10)

Notes

1. Henry van Dyke, *Story of the Other Wise Man* (Paraclete Press, 1984).
2. Paul Lawrence Dunbar, *Theology*.
3. Richard Baxter, *The Saints' Everlasting Rest* (New York: The American Tract Society, 1758).
4. Thomas Fuller, *Gnomologia* (1650).
5. John Milton, *Paradise Lost* (Buccaneer Books, 1983).
6. William Blake, *The First Book of Urizen* (Dover Publications, 1997).
7. Thomas Moore, *Come, Ye Disconsolate.*

12

Your Personal Journey Into Eternity

Imagine your feelings if one day you found yourself destitute of money, without employment, about to become homeless, and hungry. Then, imagine at that moment of your greatest despair, a message arrives from a lawyer informing you that a distant relative had passed away and left you an inheritance of over a million dollars, a sumptuous home, and a car. Your new good fortune would cause your despondency and depression to quickly be replaced with joy and happiness. Your formerly bleak and hopeless world would appear in an entirely new light as you considered your transformed condition.

Those who have lived without hope and have despaired at the approach of death will experience a similar transformation when they begin to understand the glorious promises of God concerning their future eternal life in Paradise when the Lord takes them home to the heavenly city of God. When we begin to appreciate the enormity of the inheritance that the Lord has prepared in Paradise for those who love Him, our conception of this life and the one to come are transformed forever. We will discover a new joy that will free us from the despair of earthly concerns.

One of the greatest glories of Heaven is eternal freedom from sickness, pain, and disease. Here on earth, we live most of our lives in fear of or suffering from pain, disease, and death. The apostle Paul understood our earthly existence in "the bondage of corruption" since the fall of Adam and Eve. He wrote, "Because the creature itself also shall be delivered from the bondage of corruption into the glorious liberty of the children of God. For we know that the whole creation groaneth and travaileth in pain together until now" (Romans 8:21–22). Imagine the pure joy of finally realizing the glorious promise of God that all disease and pain will be banished forever from our future life in the heavenly city. In the book of Revelation the prophet John revealed the wonderful promise of God regarding our future life in Heaven. "God shall wipe away all tears from their eyes; and there shall be no more death, neither sorrow, nor crying, neither shall there be any more pain: for the former things are passed away" (Revelations 21:4).

Throughout history most of humanity has worked without significant reward or rest from their labor. But, one of the great promises of God regarding our future home in Heaven is that there we will finally rest forever in perfect peace and joy. John reveals in his prophecy that our eternal life will be characterized by activity but that we will never again have to "labor" for our daily bread or existence: "And I heard a voice from Heaven saying unto me, Write, Blessed are the dead which die in the Lord from henceforth: Yea, saith the Spirit, that they may rest from their labours; and their works do follow them" (Revelation 14:13).

The Scripture's promise that death itself will be banished forever is one of the greatest victories of all. For thousands of years mankind has lived with the fear of death, and its capacity to destroy our life, our family, and our greatest plans for the future. Perhaps the greatest gift of salvation is that Jesus Christ has defeated death forever by His resurrection from the grave. The apostle Paul wrote concerning Christ's victory over death and sin: "O death, where is thy sting? O grave, where is thy victory? The sting of death is sin; and the strength of sin is the law. But thanks be to God, which giveth us the victory through our Lord Jesus Christ" (1 Corinthians 15:55–57).

From the moment our first parents were exiled from the Garden of Eden because of their rebellion against God, humanity has suffered from the curse of sin and its terrible consequences throughout history. Sin is the true curse of this world. It is the destroyer of families and lives. Moses wrote, "And the Lord said . . . the imagination of man's heart is evil from his youth" (Genesis 8:21). Every evil in this life is derived from the sinful rebellion of humans who continually succumb to the temptations of Satan. The greatest truth about our eternal life in Heaven is that we will finally enjoy perfect freedom from the bondage of sin and evil. Can you imagine what life would be like if we were to be forever free from temptation and the power of sin and evil to destroy our trust and love? The book of Revelation declares that sin and evil will never exist in the New Jerusalem. "And there shall in no wise enter into it any thing that defileth, neither whatsoever worketh abomination, or maketh a lie:

but they which are written in the Lamb's book of life" (Revelation 21:27).

Since the beginning of man's existence we have suffered under the curse of sin and evil that followed naturally from Adam and Eve's rebellion against God's law. For thousands of years humans have continued to sow the seeds of sin, lust, and greed in the earth in fulfilment of that ancient curse of sin, and reap the pain. What joy to know that the curse of sin will end forever when Christ begins His rule following the defeat of Satan: "And there shall be no more curse: but the throne of God and of the Lamb shall be in it; and his servants shall serve him" (Revelation 22:3).

The New Jerusalem

The ancient walled city of Jerusalem has a special place in both the heart of God and in His people of faith. It is mentioned in 764 verses in the Bible. Whenever I travel to Jerusalem I am overwhelmed with the feeling that I am walking on "holy ground." The most profound spiritual events in human history have unfolded in the holy city of Jerusalem. Four thousand years ago the patriarch Abraham worshipped and gave tithes to the mysterious King of Salem, Melchisedek. Beginning with the strange story of the binding of Isaac by his father Abraham in "the land of Moriah," this ancient city of Jerusalem has been the location of the most critical events in the spiritual history of humanity. After the conquest of the city by King David and the building of the glorious Temple of Jerusalem by his son King Solomon, this city became the focus of the worship of all Israelites. Three times every year all adult male Jews travelled to Jerusalem to worship God in their Temple. Jesus as Messiah-King made His entrance into the holy city through the Eastern Gate into the Temple of God.

For thousands of years the Lord met with His people in this sacred city on the sacred Temple Mount. Yet, special as it has always been, the heavenly New Jerusalem surpasses the glory of the earthly Jerusalem as the sun surpasses the moon. Even now, God is preparing the heavenly city to receive the saved of all generations. There we will live eternally. In the gospel of John, Christ prophesied to His disciples that He would prepare the New Jerusalem, the city of God, for all of His followers when He returned to Heaven. "In my Father's house are many mansions: if it were not so, I would have told you. I go to prepare a place for you" (John 14:2). Considering the glorious wonder, complexity, and beauty of this earth, which the Lord created in six days, could our minds even comprehend what must be the glory of the heavenly city, the New Jerusalem, which our Lord has created over the last two thousand years for those who love Him.

The apostle John was the only one of Jesus' original twelve disciples to live to an old age. John did not escape persecution however. He was one of the many followers of Jesus whom the Roman Emperor Domitian exiled in an attempt to stop the growth of Christianity. John's place of banishment was Patmos, an island off the coast of Turkey. On the island prison of Patmos, John recorded the prophecies of the endtimes, as revealed to him by God that has become the book of Revelation. The word "Revelation," also called "the Apocalypse," means "to break through" or reveal something previously hidden. One part of John's truly extraordinary vision of things to come is his description of the New Jerusalem, the heavenly city of God: "And I saw a new Heaven and a new earth, for the first Heaven and the first earth had passed away. Also there was no more sea. Then I, John, saw the holy city, New Jerusalem, coming down out of Heaven from God, prepared as a bride adorned for her husband" (Revelation 21:1–2).

Heaven is the eternal home of God and the great host of angels. The Bible never reveals the exact location of Heaven. Many suggest that Heaven must exist in another dimension. However, the Scriptures always describe the location of Heaven as being in a direction described as "up" and "in the north." Astronomers have determined that the direction "north" is in the direction of the Polar Star. Some Christian astronomers believe that Heaven may exist in our own dimension but that it may be light years away from the earth. The New Jerusalem is located in Heaven now. The New Jerusalem, the capital city of Heaven, is also called "paradise" in the book of Revelation: "To him that overcometh will I give to eat of the tree of life, which is in the midst of the paradise of God" (Revelation 2:7). The apostle Paul reveals that the "third Heaven" is identical to "Paradise" and the New Jerusalem. Paul wrote, "And I knew such a man, (whether in the body, or out of the body, I cannot tell: God knoweth;) How that he was caught up into paradise, and heard unspeakable words, which it is not lawful for a man to utter" (2 Corinthians 12:3–4).

A New Heaven and a New Earth

After the Millennium concludes, with God's total defeat of Satan's host, the New Jerusalem will descend to the new earth, where it will take its place among many new cities on the new earth; but it will not be like the other cities. It will always be a very special place, the home of the Bride of Christ. But before that can happen, both Heaven and the earth must be purified of all sin, to prepare them for their future role as the holy home of the Jews and Gentiles under the rule of the Messiah. The Bible says that this purification from the pollution of sin will be accomplished by fire.

"Purify the heavens?" you may ask. Yes, remember, a part of the heavens is still open today to Satan, who stands before God to accuse us before the Throne of God "day and night" (Revelation 12:10). Job's Accuser (Satan) appeared before the Throne of God to accuse him (Job 1:6–12). After the Millennium, the Accuser, Satan himself, will be "cast into the lake of fire and brimstone where the Beast and the False Prophet are. And they will be tormented day and night forever and ever" (Revelation 20:10). Sin will never exist again in the eternal new Heaven and new earth.

Thousands of years ago, during the days of Noah, God cleansed the earth with water because "the earth also was corrupt before God, and the earth was filled with violence" (Genesis 6:11). This time He will cleanse the earth by fire: "The world that then existed perished, being flooded with water. But the heavens and the earth which are now preserved by the same word, are reserved for fire until the day of judgment and perdition of ungodly men . . . the heavens will pass away with a great noise, and the elements will melt with fervent heat; both the earth and the works that are in it will be burned up" (2 Peter 3:6–7, 10).

The Heavenly City

The book of Hebrews declared that the patriarch Abraham left Ur of the Chaldees not just in search of the land of Canaan but he was spiritually looking for the city of God — the New Jerusalem. "By faith Abraham, when he was called to go out into a place which he should after receive for an inheritance, obeyed; and he went out, not knowing whither he went. By faith he sojourned in the land of promise, as in a strange country, dwelling in tabernacles with Isaac and

Jacob, the heirs with him of the same promise: For he looked for a city which hath foundations, whose builder and maker is God" (Hebrews 11:8–10).

Hebrews tells us that the great saints of the Old Testament and the martyrs of the faith were all searching for the heavenly city. "These all died in faith, not having received the promises, but having seen them afar off, and were persuaded of them, and embraced them, and confessed that they were strangers and pilgrims on the earth. For they that say such things declare plainly that they seek a country. And truly, if they had been mindful of that country from whence they came out, they might have had opportunity to have returned. But now they desire a better country, that is, an heavenly: wherefore God is not ashamed to be called their God: for he hath prepared for them a city" (Hebrews 11:13–16).

The prophet John saw this heavenly city in a vision from God, the details of which are written in the book of Revelation. The New Jerusalem is a city filled with the glory of God's divine Presence, which causes the whole city to glow with an internal light like a beautiful "jasper stone, clear as crystal" (Revelation 21:11). It is a real city, having dimensions, gates, mansions, streets and inhabitants. John used the only language at his command to describe the wonderful city that God is preparing for His people. He said the city, "is laid out as a square, and its length is as great as its breadth. And he measured the city with the reed; twelve thousand furlongs. Its length, breadth, and height are equal. Then he measured its wall; one hundred and forty-four cubits, according to the measure of a man that is, of an angel" (Revelation 21:16–17). The size of the New Jerusalem is tremendous: 1,500 miles by 1,500 miles by 1,500 miles (12,000 furlongs). "Its wall: one hundred and forty-four cubits (216 feet). . . . And the construction of its wall was of jasper" (vv. 17–18).

Can you visualize such a city? There are two possible three-dimensional shapes that correspond to this description. One is a cube and the other is a pyramid. The pyramid is probable since the city wall, with twelve gates, is 216 feet high. It is hard to visualize a cube-shaped object of that size having a wall 216 feet high around it. However, a pyramid-shaped city of that size could have a base 216 feet high with twelve gates through which the people would enter. Architects have calculated that the enormous size of the New Jerusalem would easily provide a mansion of over a half mile in length and breadth for every believer from Adam to the present. Supporting the jasper wall are twelve layers of stone foundation; on each layer "were the names of the twelve apostles of the Lamb" (v. 14). The walls have "three gates on the east, three gates on the north, three gates on the south, and three gates on the west . . . each individual gate was of one pearl" (vv. 13, 21). "The foundations of the wall of the city were adorned with all kinds of precious stones: the first foundation was jasper, the second sapphire, the third chalcedony, the fourth emerald, the fifth sardonyx, the sixth sardius, the seventh chrysolite, the eighth beryl, the ninth topaz, the tenth chrysoprase, the eleventh jacinth, and the twelfth amethyst" (vv. 19, 20). John then says "the street of the city was pure gold, like transparent glass" (v. 21).

Years ago it was almost impossible to imagine this description. Yet in nearly every major city, great skyscrapers are built today with walls of glass that appear to transform the building into gold in the sunset. One modern construction device is to apply a very thin sheet of gold to the outside glass and metal of these gigantic towers. When the sunlight hits it, the whole building appears to glow. Yet when you look directly through the golden windows from the inside, you can see that they are transparent glass. This technique not only gives a beautiful appearance to the building, it also provides excellent heat control and conservation. If man can create earthly buildings like this to reflect the glory of the earthly sun, think how magnificent the New Jerusalem will be when it reflects the glory of the Son of God. Earth's most sought after mineral, gold, will be so plentiful in the New Jerusalem that John described the streets and city as "transparent gold." The Light of God will illuminate the city of the saints for eternity.

John "saw no temple in it, for the Lord God Almighty and the Lamb are its temple" (v. 22). While the Bible does describe a temple in Heaven, the New Jerusalem will not have a Temple because God Himself will dwell with us. This reminds us of what Jesus said to the woman at the well when she challenged Him about the proper place to worship God. "Woman, believe Me, the hour is coming when you will neither on this mountain, nor in Jerusalem, worship the Father. . . . But the hour is coming, and now is, when the true worshipers will worship the Father in spirit and truth; for the Father is seeking such to worship Him. God is Spirit, and those who worship Him must worship in spirit and truth" (John 4:21–23). The very Spirit of God will pervade the entire New Jerusalem so there will be no need for a special building such as a temple. The glowing golden light of the city was "the glory of God . . . and the Lamb. And the nations of those who are saved shall walk in its light, and the kings of the earth bring their glory and honor into it" (Revelation 21:23–24). Although the Bible describes the continuation of the sun and moon in the new earth, there will be no need of either to provide light in the New Jerusalem because "there shall be no night there" (Revelation 21:25). The presence of God internally lights the whole city. Since there is no night and no danger of an enemy besieging the city, the "gates shall not be shut" (v. 25).

We will no longer be subject to the curse that God put on the earth after Adam's sin. There will be no rust or decay because the very process of entropy, the running down of the universe, will cease. When the curse of sin is removed, decay, germs and decomposition will also be eliminated. Nothing "that defiles, or causes an abomination or a lie" (Revelation 21:27) will ever enter there, though the gates are left open. The angels of God will guard the city forever.

Only those who are "white as snow" (Isaiah 1:18) because of the blood of Jesus Christ, whose names "are written in the Lamb's Book of Life" (Revelation 21:27) will inhabit the New Jerusalem.

Living in the City of God

The New Jerusalem in Heaven is now inhabited by the angels, the spirits of those who died in Christ, and those Old Testament saints who were raised from the dead as part of the firstfruits of the first resurrection. Matthew writes, "and the graves were opened; and many bodies of the saints who had fallen asleep were raised; and coming out of the graves after His resurrection, they went into the holy city and appeared to many" (Matthew 27:52–53). These resurrected saints ascended into Heaven with Jesus. At the Rapture, the spirits of those departed saints, who are already in the New Jerusalem, will receive their resurrected bodies, because the "dead in Christ" rise first. Immediately after that, we "who are alive and remain" will be transformed into our new bodies. Jesus told the Church that He was going away to prepare a place for us ". . . that where I am, there you may be also" (John 14:3). That place is the New Jerusalem in Heaven.

The Old Testament saints who were not part of the firstfruits of the resurrection when Christ arose will also be there. Paul says that these saints "all died in faith, not having received the promises, but having seen them afar off. . . . But now they desire a better, that is, a heavenly country. Therefore God is not ashamed to be called their God, for He has prepared a city for them" (Hebrews 11:13,16).

The book of Hebrews reassures the Church, the Bride of Christ, that we too will come to "the city of the living God, the heavenly Jerusalem, to an innumerable company of angels, to the general assembly and church of the firstborn who are registered in Heaven, to God the Judge of all, to the spirits of just men made perfect, to Jesus the Mediator of the new covenant" (Hebrews 12:22–24). In Philippians 4:3 Paul speaks of the day when we will be reunited with those "whose names are in the Book of Life." John, speaking of the city that has "no need of the sun or the moon," says that "there shall by no means enter it [the New Jerusalem] anything that defiles, or causes an abomination or a lie, but only those who are written in the Lamb's Book of Life" (Revelation 21:23, 27). The sole qualification to be named in the Book of Life is our acceptance of the pardon of sin offered by the Father to all who will accept His Son as their Lord and Savior.

The New Jerusalem Will Descend to Earth

Although the New Jerusalem will be the final home of all the righteous sons of God, from Adam to the last member of the Church, the members of the Bride of Christ will not be restricted to the heavenly city. We will go in and out of the gates, exploring the new earth and the new Heaven, ruling and reigning with Christ. We shall have access to the "pure river of water of life, clear as crystal, proceeding from the throne of God and of the Lamb" (Revelation 22:1). The Tree of Life, which was removed from Earth after Adam sinned, will stand near the river and will bear "twelve fruits, each tree yielding its fruit every month" (v. 2). We will have fruit to eat in the New Jerusalem. The mention of months and seasons shows that we will undoubtedly have a variety of climate conditions. We will be able to approach "the throne of God and the Lamb" and will serve Him. We "shall see His face, and His name shall be on [our] foreheads" (vv. 3–4).

John must have been thrilled as he heard a loud voice from Heaven saying, "Behold, the tabernacle of God is with men, and He will dwell with them, and they shall be His people, and God Himself will be with them and be their God. And God will wipe away every tear from their eyes; there shall be no more death, nor sorrow, nor crying. There shall be no more pain, for the former things have passed away" (Revelation 21:3–4).

From His throne God declared, "It is done! I am the Alpha and the Omega, the Beginning and the End. I will give of the fountain of the water of life freely to him who thirsts. He who overcomes shall inherit all things, and I will be his God and he shall be my son" (Revelation 21:6–7). But in the midst of this glorious promise is a note of warning: "He who overcomes shall inherit all things, and I will be his God and he shall be My son. But the cowardly, unbelieving, abominable, murderers, sexually immoral, sorcerers, idolaters, and all liars shall have their part in the lake which burns with fire and brimstone, which is the second death" (Revelation 21: 7–8). John ends the Book of Revelation with, "And the Spirit and the bride say, 'Come!'

And let him who hears say, 'Come!' And let him who thirsts come. Whoever desires, let him take the water of life freely. . . . Surely I come quickly.' Amen. Even so, come, Lord Jesus!" (Revelation 22:17–20).

Rewards of Jesus Christ to Faithful Servants

> And, behold, I come quickly; and my reward is with me, to give every man according as his work shall be. I am Alpha and Omega, the beginning and the end, the first and the last. Blessed are they that do his commandments, that they may have right to the tree of life, and may enter in through the gates into the city. (Revelation 22:12–14)

The prophet John was given a vision of the final Great Judgment of the wicked dead that will take place at the end of the age. Throughout history both poets and painters have portrayed this final Judgment Day as one single judgment before the Throne of God in which all of humanity, both saints and sinners, including all of the living and dead, would be judged together at one time before Almighty God. However, the Bible reveals there are several separate judgments of God in which He will judge all who have ever lived. If we wish to understand the justice of God, we must examine what the Scriptures reveal about these seven judgments.

All those who placed their faith and trust in Christ have had their personal sin judged and dealt with forever at the Cross according to the holy law of God. The Bible assures us that "the wages of sin are death" and therefore, it was necessary that Jesus Christ die on the cross and bear the eternal punishment for our evil rebellion. This judgment occurred almost two thousand years ago on Calvary. But its benefits are applied today to the hearts of men and women when they personally believe in Christ and accept God's pardon based on the perfect atonement of the Cross.

"Now is the judgment of this world: now shall the prince of this world be cast out. And I, if I be lifted up from the earth, will draw all men unto me. This he said, signifying what death he should die" (John 12:31–33). Jesus acknowledged that the basis of this judgment is His finished and perfect atoning work on the Cross. The actual death of the sinless Son of God on the Cross and the gift of eternal life in Heaven opened the way to all people to accept this pardon from God.

The Lord describes a continuing judgment of our daily walk by the Holy Spirit awakening our conscience to an active obedience to the will of God. "For if we would judge ourselves, we should not be judged. But when we are judged, we are chastened of the Lord, that we should not be condemned with the world" (1 Corinthians 11:31–32). The chastening of God is a mark of His manifested love for us. Its purpose is to redirect us to an even closer walk with Him. While we often resent this chastening, just as children resent the chastening of their parents, it is done out of a profound love for us and a desire for our best interests. In the book of Hebrews 12:11, Paul assures us of the lasting value of these painful chastening experiences: "Now no chastening for the present seemeth to be joyous, but grievous: nevertheless afterward it yieldeth the peaceable fruit of righteousness unto them which are exercised thereby."

The Final Judgment of Unrepentant Sinners

> And I saw a great white throne, and him that sat on it, from whose face the earth and the Heaven fled away; and there was found no place for them. And I saw

> the dead, small and great, stand before God; and the books were opened: and another book was opened, which is the book of life: and the dead were judged out of those things which were written in the books, according to their works. And the sea gave up the dead which were in it; and death and Hell delivered up the dead which were in them: and they were judged every man according to their works. And death and Hell were cast into the lake of fire. This is the second death. And whosoever was not found written in the book of life was cast into the lake of fire. (Revelation 20:11–15)

The Great White Throne Judgment for all unrepentant sinners from the creation of Adam will occur in Heaven after the Millennium. This judgment will also include the final judgment of all the rebellious angels, the "sons of God," who rebelled against God in the distant past. Since it will occur in Heaven after the Millennium, all unrepentant men and women who have lived since Adam until that point will stand before the Throne of God. The prophet John described earlier the Battle of Armageddon and the defeat of Satan. He is chained in the bottomless pit for a period of one thousand years, which allows mankind to enjoy the peace and prosperity of the Kingdom of God. John prophesied that, after the Millennium, Satan would be released to lead a final rebellion against God. He would then be cast into the lake of fire forever. Immediately after that, John tells us, the final judgment of wicked angels and men will take place in Heaven.

The wicked angels who joined in Satan's initial rebellion against God will stand before the Great White Throne. These rebellious angels belong to two groups. The first group includes the fallen angels who sinned in a particular manner before the Flood and entered into sexual relations with women. They were imprisoned by God in a special place where they will be held until the day of the Great White Throne Judgment. "For if God spared not the angels that sinned, but cast them down to Hell, and delivered them into chains of darkness, to be reserved unto judgment" (2 Peter 2:4). The book of Jude confirms that these fallen angels violated God's law against sexual contact between angelic beings and humans. "And the angels which kept not their first estate, but left their own habitation, he hath reserved in everlasting chains under darkness unto the judgment of the great day. Even as Sodom and Gomorrha, and the cities about them in like manner, giving themselves over to fornication, and going after strange flesh, are set forth for an example, suffering the vengeance of eternal fire" (Jude 6–7). The second group of rebellious angels who did not sin in that way were allowed to follow Satan. On Judgment Day they will be imprisoned forever in the lake of "everlasting fire, prepared for the devil and his angels" (Matthew 25:41). Note that in this passage Christ says that the lake of fire was originally prepared for the devil and his angels. If man had never rebelled against God or if all men had repented of their sins, then the gates of Hell would never have opened to mankind.

The purpose of the dreaded Great White Throne Judgment is to give every man a fair trial before God the Father and Jesus Christ. The Psalmist King David states, "But the Lord shall endure for ever: he hath prepared his throne for judgment. And he shall judge the world in righteousness, he shall minister judgment to the people in uprightness" (Psalm 9:7–8). The souls of all men who have died in their sins will be given resurrected bodies for that ultimate judgment day. The Bible says that the grave and even the sea will give up their bodies and Hell will surrender their souls so that they can stand before Jesus. "And I saw the dead, small and great, stand before God; and the books were opened: and another book was opened, which is the book of life: and the dead were judged out of those things which were written in the books, according to their works" (Revelation 20:12). All those who appear at this judgment will be judged by the works and deeds of their individual lives. When the "books are opened" every soul present before the judgment seat of God will be proven to have rebelliously sinned against God, demonstrated by the fact that their name cannot be found in "the Book of Life," that each of them had failed to repent of their sins. When the books that record the works of men are opened, every secret thought and deed will be revealed once and for all. The life and deeds of every lost soul will stand in judgment against them on that last day. Those who refuse Christ's offer of salvation in this life will find themselves standing before the throne of God's judgment in the next life.

Revelation 20:12 describes that tragic final moment when sinners will stand before God without any further excuse or means of evading their coming judgment. Then, "another book [is] opened, which is the book of life." The Book of Life contains only the names of those who have secured eternal life because they accepted the pardon of Jesus Christ for their sinful rebellion. The tragic reason that the Book of Life must be opened on that awful judgment day when only unrepentant sinners will stand before God is because many will, even then, falsely claim to be Christians. They will point to their public religious life and their words, but God will point to their heart and the Book of Life where their name will not be found. Jesus warned His listeners that in that final day He would examine their heart, not their outward works.

"Not every one that saith unto me, Lord, Lord, shall enter into the kingdom of Heaven; but he that doeth the will of my Father which is in Heaven. Many will say to me in that day, Lord, Lord, have we not prophesied in thy name? and in thy name have cast out devils? and in thy name done many wonderful works? And then will I profess unto them, I never knew you: depart from me, ye that work iniquity" (Matthew 7:21–23).

Throughout history man-made religions have vainly attempted to win the favor of God by accomplishing good works or religious deeds. People vainly hope their righteous deeds will make them acceptable to a Holy God on the final day of judgment and enable them to live forever in a holy Heaven. Some people are offended by the simplicity of the Gospel of salvation by faith alone in Jesus' sacrifice. It appeals to the spiritual pride of humanity to achieve their own salvation by somehow deserving God's favor. The tragic flaw in this theory is that no amount of good works will ever erase the sinful rebellion which exists in the heart of every son of Adam. As Paul wrote, "Therefore by the deeds of the law there shall no flesh be justified in his sight. . . . Therefore we conclude that a man is justified by faith without the deeds of the law" (Romans 3:20, 28). The only cure for our sin and our guilt is to be miraculously transformed by the blood of Jesus Christ into that perfect righteousness which alone makes us acceptable to God and fit for an eternity in Heaven. Those who reject the only plan of salvation offered by God will be judged and sentenced to an eternity without God.

Jesus promised His followers that we too will be judged after our life on earth is through. However, this judgment will not involve punishment because our sins were covered forever by Christ's completed sacrifice on the cross.

> But why dost thou judge thy brother? or why dost thou set at nought thy brother? for we shall all stand before the judgment seat of Christ. For it is written, As I live, saith the Lord, every knee shall bow to me, and every tongue shall confess to God. So then every one of us shall give account of himself to God. (Romans 14:10–12)

The judgment of all Christian believers will take place in Heaven before Jesus Christ. Paul wrote, "for we shall all stand before the judgment seat of Christ" (Romans 14:10). This will occur in Heaven, apparently immediately after the Rapture of the Church. Christ will reward our faithful service to God. This judgment will not adversely affect anyone's personal salvation because only those souls who were saved by the blood of Jesus Christ will appear at this judgment. The apostle Paul uses the Greek word *bema* to describe this judgment of believers. The word *bema* is derived from the crown or wreath that the city judges gave to a victorious athlete after a tournament. The Scriptures teach that all Christians will be judged by Jesus on the basis of their righteous works or the lack of such deeds.

The apostle Paul wrote:

> For other foundation can no man lay than that is laid, which is Jesus Christ. Now if any man build upon this foundation gold, silver, precious stones, wood, hay, stubble; Every man's work shall be made manifest: for the day shall declare it, because it shall be revealed by fire; and the fire shall try every man's work of what sort it is. If any man's work abide

> which he hath built thereupon, he shall receive a reward. If any man's work shall be burned, he shall suffer loss: but he himself shall be saved; yet so as by fire. (1 Corinthians 3:12–15)

Those believers whose lives have revealed true spiritual gold and silver will receive eternal rewards in Heaven. Those whose lives reveal only spiritual "wood and stubble," the temporary and personally motivated spiritual acts, will not receive the great rewards and crowns of glory. But they will still be saved by the blood of Christ. We are saved by the atoning finished work of Christ applied to our heart, not by our subsequent works. However, the Lord has promised eternal rewards for those who have lived in holiness and obedience to His commands.

Every believer will have an opportunity to qualify for positions of leadership in the world to come through our faithful obedience to Christ today. To reign and rule with Christ is part of the reward that will belong to Christians in the Millennium on the new earth. Prophecies reveal that King David will be resurrected as the king of Israel, in a special position as prince-regent in Jerusalem, with Jesus Christ the Messiah ruling as the King of Kings. The disciples of Christ will rule the twelve tribes of Israel. "And Jesus said unto them, Verily I say unto you, That ye which have followed me, in the regeneration when the Son of man shall sit in the throne of his glory, ye also shall sit upon twelve thrones, judging the twelve tribes of Israel" (Matthew 19:28). The book of Revelation declares, "Blessed and holy is he that hath part in the first resurrection: on such the second death hath no power, but they shall be priests of God and of Christ, and shall reign with him a thousand years" (Revelation 20:6).

Many Christians will be appointed as rulers of various cities and territories throughout the world under the overall rule of the Messiah from the throne of David in Jerusalem. Jesus taught us that our future responsibilities and duties in ruling the world will reflect the faithfulness in our Christian walk. In his parable of the faithful and unfaithful servants, Jesus illustrated that our faithfulness will determine our future position. In the parable the master "said unto him, Well, thou good servant: because thou hast been faithful in a very little, have thou authority over ten cities" (Luke 19:17).

Other leadership roles will belong to faithful Christians. These positions of leadership will be given as a reward to those whose spiritual life has reflected the fruits of the Spirit and the true spiritual gold and silver. While we are saved by the blood of Christ, we will not earn the right to rule simply by accepting salvation: "Every man's work shall be made manifest: for the day shall declare it, because it shall be revealed by fire; and the fire shall try every man's work of what sort it is. If any man's work abide which he hath built thereupon, he shall receive a reward. If any man's work shall be burned, he shall suffer loss: but he himself shall be saved; yet so as by fire" (1 Corinthians 3:13–15).

The Eternal Rewards for Believers

We are told in the great chapter of faith, Hebrews 11:24–26 that we should be motivated in our daily walk before Christ by an awareness of the final reward that awaits all faithful believers. "By faith Moses, when he was come to years, refused to be called the son of Pharaoh's daughter; Choosing rather to suffer affliction with the people of God, than to enjoy the pleasures of sin for a season; Esteeming the reproach of Christ greater riches than the treasures in

Egypt: for he had respect unto the recompense of the reward." The motive of Moses in rejecting the pleasures of Egyptian royalty for the persecution of following God was his understanding of the tremendous eternal reward that God offered to all believers. Our eternal life in Heaven will reveal a hierarchy of rewards and glory that reflects our faithfulness to Christ. Although our salvation is solely dependent upon the completed atonement of Christ, there are rewards that will be enjoyed forever for those who follow the Lord in obedience and holiness.

One of the major reasons for the lack of holiness and faithful dedication to Christ in the Church today is that many people have lost sight of the rewards of Heaven. We often hear the saying, "We can become so heavenly minded that we are no earthy good." The tragedy in the Church today is the opposite error. We have become so earthly minded that we are in serious danger of being no heavenly good. One of my motivations in this study is to help restore a proper balance in our outlook and to re-emphasize the reality and promises of our heavenly rewards as we follow Christ. Thomas à Kempis, the author of *Imitation of Christ*, wrote, "In Heaven, to be even the least is a great thing, where all will be great; for all shall be called the children of God."

Many followers of Jesus Christ work for the Lord in almost total obscurity in foreign missions, ghetto medical centers, and pioneering churches. They will never receive public gratitude, honors, or even the quiet acknowledgment of other Christians or Church leaders in this life for their righteous works. There are millions of faithful servants of God who will go to their graves without receiving any positive reward in this life, but in Heaven Jesus will honor these Christians with crowns and rewards for their service to Him. Those who "have fought the good fight" will receive the rewards and heavenly justice that may have eluded them in this earthly life.

One of the curious facts about almost all earthly goals and rewards is that, once we have achieved them, their attraction seems to gradually fade away. Those trophies that we won with such great effort and pride eventually tarnish and are put away in a closet because the nature of all earthly awards is fleeting. The unique nature of the heavenly crowns and rewards that Jesus Christ will offer to faithful saints on Judgment Day is that they will never fade away nor tarnish throughout eternity. Those who win these rewards from Christ will wear their glorious crowns of honor forever in Heaven. A trillion years from today the crowned saint will meet other Christians, including the great heroes of the faith from the Scriptures, and will know that everyone will see at a glance that they have won a great reward from their Lord and Savior. No temporary reward in this life could possibly compare to the eternal rewards that God offers those who are faithful.

Jesus Christ promised a "crown of life" to every believer who withstood the trials and tribulations, including those who endured martyrdom for Christ. In Revelation God promises, "Be thou faithful unto death, and I will give thee a crown of life" (Revelation 2:10). Those who hate the Gospel believe that the Christian will lose his life and everything worthwhile when they face martyrdom for their faith. However, in the world to come, those who were willing to follow Christ to the point of death will receive the glorious martyr's crown of life. They will be honored in Heaven forever.

Elders, teachers, deacons, and pastors in the Church who have faithfully and unselfishly served Jesus Christ will receive a crown of glory as their reward from God: "The elders which are among you I exhort, who am also an elder, and a witness of the sufferings of Christ, and also a partaker of the glory that shall be revealed: Feed the flock of God which is among you, taking the oversight thereof, not by constraint, but willingly; not for filthy lucre, but of a ready mind; And when the chief Shepherd shall appear, ye shall receive a crown of glory that fadeth not away" (1 Peter 5:1–2, 4).

Christians who have won others to faith in Jesus Christ as their Savior are promised a "crown of rejoicing" as a special reward in Heaven. In the same manner in which society today offers honors to those who save people from a burning house, we are promised that God will honor those who have faithfully witnessed to their friends and neighbors about Christ. "For what is our hope, or joy, or crown of rejoicing? Are not even ye in the presence of our Lord Jesus Christ at his coming?" (1 Thessalonians 2:19). Our increased understanding of the biblical truths about Heaven and Hell should motivate us to share our faith with others concerning salvation through Jesus Christ.

A "crown of righteousness" will be given to all Christians who long for the return of Christ. Too many Christians today are so caught up in their own life plans that they have lost sight of the glorious truth that Jesus is going to return soon to set up His kingdom. "Henceforth there is laid up for me a crown of righteousness, which the Lord, the righteous judge, shall give me at that day: and not to me only, but unto all them also that love his appearing" (2 Timothy 4:8). Throughout the New Testament, Christians are told again and again to be watchful for the imminent return of their Lord and Savior. While we must be watchful, we are also told to occupy until He comes. We must live in a spiritually creative tension in which we should plan as though we have a hundred years until He returns but live as though He will return before the next dawn.

There is an "incorruptible crown" of purity for the victors in the daily spiritual struggle that we wage in this life. "And every man that striveth for the mastery is temperate in all things. Now they do it to obtain a corruptible crown; but we an incorruptible" (1 Corinthians 9:25). The Bible tells us to "put on the whole armor of God, that ye may be able to stand against the wiles of the devil" (Ephesians 6:11), to be prepared for constant spiritual warfare. Paul tells us that we must exercise spiritual discipline, like an athlete, if we are to find victory in Christ. "I therefore so run, not as uncertainly; so fight I, not as one that beateth the air: But I keep under my body, and bring it into subjection . . ." (1 Corinthians 9:26-27). He uses the imagery of an athlete who practices running in preparation for a race or a boxer who prepares for a difficult fight. Paul declares that our spiritual rewards and heaven's crowns are worth the fight.

> Behold, I come quickly: hold that fast which thou hast, that no man take thy crown. Him that overcometh will I make a pillar in the temple of my God, and he shall go no more out: and I will write upon him the name of my God, and the name of the city of my God, which is new Jerusalem, which cometh down out of Heaven from my God: and I will write upon him my new name. He that hath an ear, let him hear what the Spirit saith unto the churches. (Revelation 3:11–13)

Someone once said, "I don't want justice; I want mercy." Fortunately God offers mercy to anyone who accepts forgiveness on His terms. God's great mercy is manifested to us in the offer of salvation to all who will repent of their sin and accept Jesus as their personal Savior. Then, and only then, can any of us look forward to receiving the justice of God. Those who insist on having an eternity on their own terms, rather than on God's terms, will finally receive it, but at the cost of their salvation. John Milton wrote in his epic poem *Paradise Lost* that Satan and every unrepentant soul who rejects salvation is really making a choice: "My choice to reign is worth ambition though in Hell: Better to reign in Hell, than serve in Heaven."

Jesus Christ proclaims His love and forgiveness for all those who will repent of their sin and He invites every one of us to accept His great offer of salvation found in the last words of the Bible as revealed in the book of Revelation:

> Behold, I stand at the door, and knock: if any man hear my voice, and open the door, I will come in to him, and will sup with him, and he with me. To him that overcometh will I grant to sit with me in my throne, even as I also overcame, and am set down with my Father in his throne." (Revelation 3:20–21)

Selected Bibliography

Aldwinckle, Russell. *Death in the Secular City*. Grand Rapids: William B. Eerdmans Publishing Company, 1974.

Anderson, J. N. D. *The Evidence for the Resurrection*. Downers Grove: Inter-Varsity Press, 1966.

Anderson, Sir Robert. *Human Destiny*. 8th ed. Kilmarnock: John Ritchie, Publisher of Christian Literature, 1913.

Anderson, Sir Robert. *The Lord from Heaven*. Baltimore: Trustworthy Books Company.

Ankerberg, John, and John Weldon. *The Facts on Life after Death*. Eugene: Harvest House Publishers, 1992.

Armstrong, Amzi. *Lectures on the Visions of the Revelation*. Morristown: P. A. Johnson, 1815.

Atwater, P. M. H. *Beyond the Light*. New York: Avon Books, 1995.

Aviezer, Nathan. *In the Beginning*. Hoboken: KTAV Publishing House, Inc., 1995.

Barnes, Rev. Albert. *Notes on the Book of Revelation*. Edinburgh: Gall & Inglis, 1852.

Bickersteth, Rev. E. H. *Hades and Heaven*. New York: Hurst & Company.

Blackmore, Susan. *Beyond the Body*. Chicago: Chicago Academy Publishers, 1992.

Blackmore, Susan. *Dying to Live*. Buffalo: Prometheus Books, 1993.

Bloomfield, Arthur, E. *A Survey of Bible Prophecy*. Minneapolis: Bethany Fellowship, Inc., 1971.

Boston, Thomas. *Human Nature in Its Fourfold State*. Philadelphia: Ambrose Walker, 1814.

Bounds, E. M. *Catching a Glimpse of Heaven*. Springdale: Whitaker House, 1985.

Bounds, Rev. Edward. *The Ineffable Glory*. New York: George H. Doran Company, 1921.

Boyd, Robert. *The World's Hope*. Chicago: J. W. Goodspeed, 1873.

Buck, Rev. Charles. *A Theological Dictionary*. Philadelphia: William W. Woodward, 1825.

Bullinger, E. W. *The Apocalypse or the Day of the Lord*. London: Eyre & Spottiswoode, 1909.

Camp, Norman H. *The Resurrection of the Human Body*. Chicago: The Bible Institute Colportrage Association, 1937.

Coates, C. A. *An Outline of the Revelation*. London: Stow Hill Bible Depot and Publishing Office, 1985.

Dean, I. R. *The Coming Kingdom — The Goal of Prophecy*. Philadelphia: Philadelphia School of the Bible, 1928.

Dewart, Edward Hartley. *Jesus the Messiah*. Toronto: William Briggs, 1891.

Edersheim, Rev. Alfred. *The Life and Times of Jesus the Messiah*. New York: Longmans, Green, & Co. 1896.

Editors of *Angel Voices or Words of Cousel*. Boston: Ticknor and Fields, 1864.

Edwards, Paul. *Immortality*. Amherst: Prometheus Books, 1997.

Glynn, Patrick. *God — The Evidence*. Rocklin: Forum, 1999.

Gonzalez-Wippler, Migene. *What Happens after Death*. St. Paul: Llewellyn Publications, 1997.

Graham, Dr. Billy. *Angels*. Waco: Word Books, 1975.

Greene, H. Leon. *If I Should Wake Before I Die*. Wheaton: Crossway Books, 1997.

Greenleaf, Simon. *The Testimony of the Evangelists*. Grand Rapids: Kregel Classics, 1995.

Gundry, Robert, H. *The Church and the Tribulation*. Grand Rapids: Zondervan Publishing House, 1977.

Haldeman, I. M. *The Coming of Christ*. New York: Charles C. Cook, 1906.

Harrington, Alan. *The Immortalist*. New York: Avon Books, 1970.

Hendriksen, William. *The Bible on the Life Hereafter*. Grand Rapids: Baker Book House, 1959.

Himmelfarb, Martha. *Tours of Hell*. Philadelphia: University of Pennsylvania Press, 1983.

Hovery, Alvah. *Biblical Eschatology*. Philadelphia: American Baptist Publication Society, 1888.

Hunt, Dave. *Whatever Happened to Heaven*. Eugene: Harvest House Publishers, 1988.

Ironside, H. A. *Lectures on the Book of Revelation*. New York: Loizeaux Brothers, 1930.

Jefferson, Charles Edward. *Why We May Believe in Life after Death*. Boston: Houghton Mifflin Company, 1911.

Jukes, Andrew. *The Second Death and the Restitution of All Things*. London: Longmans, Green, and Co., 1878.

Keith, Rev. Alexander. *The Signs of the Times*. Edinburgh: William White & Co., 1832.

Krailsheimer, A., and J. Pascal. *Pensees*. London: Penguin Books, 1966.

Kubler-Ross, Elisabeth. *On Death and Dying*. New York: Scribner, 1997.

Kubler-Ross, Elisabeth. *On Life After Death*. Berkeley: CelestialArts, 1991.

Kubler-Ross, Elisabeth. *The Tunnel and the Light*. New York: Marlowe & Company, 1999.

Kubler-Ross, Elisabeth. *The Wheel of Life*. New York: Touchstone, 1998.

LaHaye, Tim. *The Beginning of the End*. Wheaton: Tyndale House Publishers, 1976.

Leslie, John. *Universes.* London: Routledge, 1989.

Lewis, C. S. *A Case for Christianity*. Grand Rapids: Baker Book House, 1977.

Litt, Charles, R. H. *Studies in the Apocalypse.* Edinburgh: T. & T. Clark, 1913.

Ludwigson, R. *A Survey of Bible Prophecy*. Grand Rapids: Zondervan Publishing House, 1975.

Luibheid, Colm. *The Essential Eusebius*. Toronto: The New American Library of Canada, 1966.

Maeterlinck, Maurice. *Death.* New York: Dodd, Mead & Company, 1912.

Maimonides, Moses. *Treatise on Resurrection*. Trans. Fred Rosner. New York: KTAV Publishing House, Inc., 1982.

Malz, Betty. *Heaven, A Bright & Glorious Place*. Old Tappan: Chosen Books, 1989.

McDowell, Josh. *More Than a Carpenter*. Wheaton: Tyndale House Publishers, Inc., 1977.

Milner, Rev. Isaac. *The History of the Church of Christ*. Cambridge: John Burges, 1800.

Moffett, Samuel Hugh. *A History of Christianity in Asia*. 1 vol. Maryknoll: Orbis Books, 1998. Vol. 1.

Moody, Jr., Raymond A. *Life After Life.* New York: Bantam Books, 1978.

Moody, Jr., Raymond A. *The Light Beyond*. New York: Bantam Books, 1989.

Morse, Melvin, and Paul Perry. *Closer to the Light*. New York: Ivy Books, 1991.

Morse, Melvin, and Paul Perry. *Transformed by the Light*. New York: Ivy Books, 1994.

Myers, Frederic W. H. *Human Personality and Its Survival of Bodily Death*. London: Longmans, Green & Co., Ltd., 1927.

Newton, Bishop Thomas. *Dissertations on the Prophecies*. London: R & R Gilbert, 1817.

Nicoll, W. Robertson. *Reunion in Eternity*. New York: George H. Doran Company, 1919.

Nunn, Rev. H. P. V. *Christian Inscriptions*. Cambridge: The Sevile Press Eton, 1952.

Pentecost, Dwight J. *Things to Come*. Grand Rapids: Zondervan Publishing House, 1958.

Peters, George. *The Theocratic Kingdom*. Grand Rapids: Kregel Publications, 1957.

Peters, Madison C. *After Death — What?* New York: The Christian Herald, 1908.

Potts, Rev. J. H. *The Golden Dawn*. Philadelphia: P. W. Ziegler & Co., 1884.

Proctor, William. *The Resurrection Report*. Nashville: Broadman & Holman Publishers, 1998.

Pusey, Rev. E. B. *The Minor Prophets*. New York: Funk & Wagnalls, 1885.

Ramm, Bernard. *Them He Glorified*. Grand Rapids: Wm. B. Eerdmans Publishing Company, 1963.

Rawlings, Maurice S. *To Hell and Back*. Nashville: Thomas Nelson Publishers, 1993.

Richards, Lawrence O. *It Couldn't Just Happen*. Dallas: Word Publishing, 1989.

Riggenbach, Eduard. *The Resurrection of Jesus*. New York: Eaton & Mains, 1907.

Robertson, A. T. *Luke The Historian in the Light of Research.* New York: Charles Scribner's Sons, 1923.

Robinson, Gershon, and Mordechai Steinman. *The Obvious Proof*. New York: C.I.S. Publishers, 1993.

Rossetti, Christina. *The Face of the Deep*. London: Society For Promoting Christian Knowledge, 1895.

Russell, J. Stuart. *The Parousia*. Grand Rapids: Baker Book House, 1983.

Schroeder, Gerald L. *The Science of God*. New York: Broadway Books, 1998.

Seiss, J. A. *The Apocalypse*, Grand Rapids: Zondervan Publishing House, 1960.

Spetner, Dr. Lee M. *Not by Chance*. New York: The Judaica Press, Inc., 1998.

Stebbins, J. E. *Our Departed Friends, or Glory of the Immortal Life*. Hartford: L. Stebbins, 1867.

Steiger, Brad, and Sherry Hansen Steiger. *Children of the Light*. New York: Penguin Books, 1995.

Strobel, Lee. *The Case for Christ*. Grand Rapids: Zondervan Publishing House, 1998.

Taylor, Rev. G. F. *The Second Coming of Jesus*. Franklin Springs: The Publishing House, 1950.

Tenney, Merrill C. *Resurrection Realities.* Los Angeles: Bible House of Los Angeles, 1945.

Theissen, Gerd, and Annette Merz. *The Historical Jesus*. Minneapolis: Fortress Press, 1996.

Thompson, Rev. J. L. *That Glorious Future*. London: Morgan and Scott, 1887.

Torrey, R. A. *Get Ready for Forever*. Springdale: Whitaker House, 1985.

Tristram, Rev. H. B. *The Seven Golden Candlesticks*. London: The Religious Tract Society, 1872.

Trotter, W. *Plain Papers on Prophetic and Other Subjects*. London: G. Morrish, 1869.

Walls, Jerry L. *Hell — The Logic of Damnation*. Notre Dame: University of Notre Dame Press, 1992.

West, Gilbert. *Observations on the History and Evidences of the Resurrection of Jesus Christ*. 3rd ed. London: R. Dodsley, 1747.

White, Wilbert W. *The Resurrection Body.* New York: George H. Doran Company, 1923.

Wright, N. T. *Jesus and the Victory of God*. Minneapolis: Fortress Press, 1996.

Zaleski, Carol. *Otherworld Journeys*. New York: Oxford University Press, 1987.

JESUS THE GREAT DEBATE

Video Documentary

This fascinating video documentary explores the powerful historical, archeological, and scientific evidence that proves the Gospel record about Jesus Christ is authentic. An excellent teaching and evangelism resource for study by families, small groups, and churches.

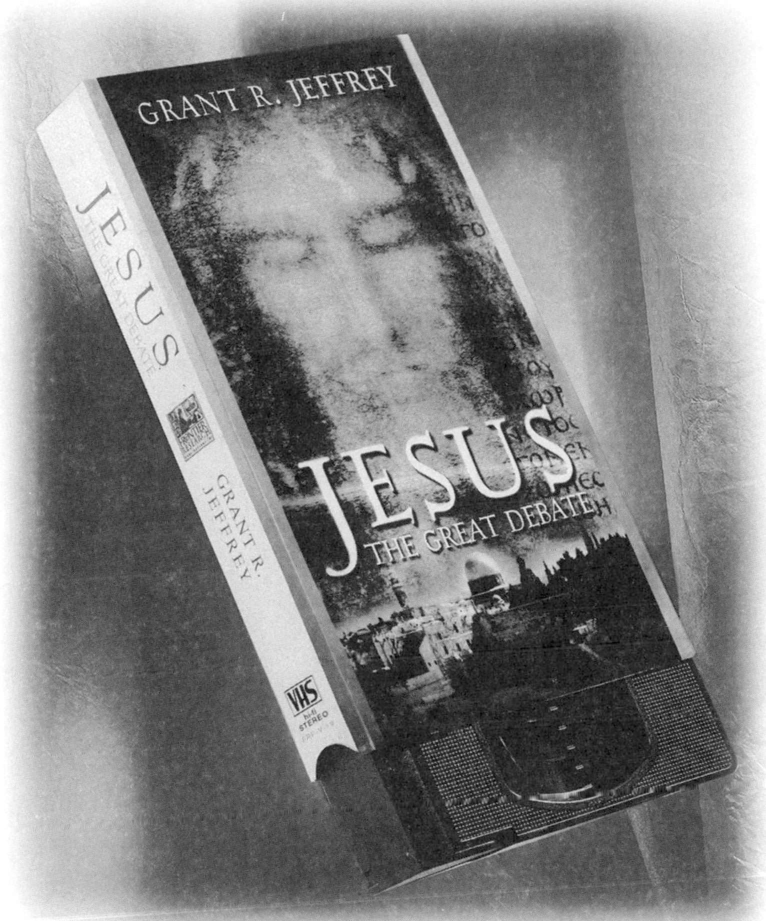

VIDEO: Retail: $19.99 • ISBN: 0-921714-39-4 • (Running Time: 60 Minutes) *Also Available* AUDIO: Retail: $15.99 • ISBN: 0-921714-41-6

AVAILABLE IN CHRISTIAN BOOKSTORES EVERYWHERE
(OR BY CALLING) IN USA: 1-800-883-1812 IN CANADA: 1-800-853-1423
www.grantjeffrey.com

(Prices may vary in Canada)

Frontier Research Publications

Grant Jeffrey Ministries

Available in Christian bookstores everywhere

Quantity	Code	Description	Price	Total
		Softback Books		
	BK-3	Messiah – War in the Middle East & The Road to Armageddon	$12.99	
	BK-4	Apocalypse – The Coming Judgment of the Nations	$12.99	
	BK-5	Prince of Darkness – Antichrist and the New World Order	$13.99	
	BK-6	Final Warning – Economic Collapse and Coming World Government	$13.99	
	BK-7	Heaven – The Mystery of Angels	$12.99	
	BK-8	The Signature of God – Astonishing Biblical Discoveries	$13.99	
	BK-9	Yeshua – The Name of Jesus Revealed in the Old Testament (Yacov Rambsel)	$11.99	
	BK-10	Armageddon – Appointment With Destiny	$12.99	
	BK-11	His Name is Jesus – The Mysterious Yeshua Codes (Yacov Rambsel)	$12.99	
	BK-12	The Handwriting of God – Sacred Mysteries of the Bible	$13.99	
	BK-14	The New World Religion (Gary H. Kah)	$12.99	
	BK-16	Jesus, The Great Debate	$13.99	
	BK-17	Image of the Risen Christ (Dr. Kenneth E. Stevenson)	$13.99	
	BK-18	Surveillance Society – The Rise of Antichrist	$13.99	
	BK-19	Journey Into Eternity – Search for Immortality	$13.99	
		ANY THREE BOOKS OR MORE **EACH**	**$11.00**	
		Hardcover Books		
	HC-H	Heaven – The Mystery of Angels	$15.99	
	W-50	Mysterious Bible Codes	$19.99	
	W-51	Flee The Darkness (Grant R. Jeffrey and Angela Hunt) *Fiction*	$17.99	
	W-52	By Dawn's Early Light (Grant R. Jeffrey and Angela Hunt) *Fiction*	$18.99	
	W-53	The Spear of Tyranny (Grant R. Jeffrey and Angela Hunt) *Fiction*	$18.99	
		Videos		
	V-5	The Rebirth of Israel and The Messiah	$19.99	
	V-6	The Antichrist and The Mark of The Beast	$19.99	
	V-7	The Rapture and Heaven's Glory	$19.99	
	V-8	The Coming Millennial Kingdom	$19.99	
	V-9	The Search for The Messiah	$19.99	
	V-13	Archeological Discoveries: Exploring Beneath the Temple Mount	$19.99	
	V-14	Prince of Darkness and The Final Inquisition	$19.99	
	V-15	Secret Agenda of The New World Order and The Tribulation	$19.99	
	V-16	Rush to Armageddon	$19.99	
		ANY TWO VIDEOS OR MORE **EACH**	**$17.00**	
	V-20	Jesus, The Great Debate	$19.99	
		Total this page (to be carried forward)		

continued overleaf